Introduction to Problem Solving

Other Books in The Math Process Standards Series

Introduction to Reasoning and Proof: Grades 3–5
(Schultz-Ferrell, Hammond, and Robles)
Introduction to Communication: Grades 3–5 (O'Connell)
Introduction to Connections: Grades 3–5 (Bamberger and Oberdorf)
Introduction to Representation: Grades 3–5 (Ennis and Witeck)

For information on the PreK–2 grades and 6–8 grades series see the Heinemann website, www.heinemann.com.

Introduction to Problem Solving

Grades 3–5

SECOND EDITION

Susan O'Connell

The Math Process Standards Series
Susan O'Connell, Series Editor

HEINEMANN
Portsmouth, NH

Heinemann
A division of Reed Elsevier Inc.
361 Hanover Street
Portsmouth, NH 03801–3912
www.heinemann.com

Offices and agents throughout the world

The authors and publisher wish to thank those who have generously given permission to reprint borrowed material:

Excerpts from *Principles and Standards for School Mathematics*. Copyright © 2000 by the National Council of Teachers of Mathematics. Reprinted with permission. All rights reserved.

Library of Congress Cataloging-in-Publication Data
O'Connell, Susan.
    Introduction to problem solving : grades 3–5 / Susan O'Connell. —2nd ed.
        p. cm.—(The math process standards series)
    Includes bibliographical references.
    ISBN-13: 978-0-325-00970-4
    ISBN-10: 0-325-00970-8
    1. Problem solving—Study and teaching (Elementary).   I. Title.
    QA63.O357 2007
    370.15′24—dc22   2006029095

Editor: Emily Michie Birch
Production: Elizabeth Valway
Cover design: Night & Day Design
Composition: Publishers' Design and Production Services, Inc.
CD production: Nicole Russell and Marla Berry
Manufacturing: Jamie Carter

Printed in the United States of America on acid-free paper
11 10 09 08 07   ML   1 2 3 4 5

To Brendan and Katie,
for the time spent solving math problems together

CONTENTS

Foreword   xi

Acknowledgments   xiii

NCTM Process Standards and Expectations   xv

Introduction   1

1   Building Math Understanding Through Problem Solving   7

Teaching Math Through Problems   8

A Look at Problem-Centered Instruction   8

Selecting Meaningful Tasks   9

The Role of Communication   10

A Look at a Problem-Based Lesson   12

Problems as a Teaching Tool   14

Questions for Discussion   15

2   Guiding Students Through the Problem-Solving Process   16

The Problem-Solving Process   16

Breaking Down the Process   17

Recording Steps in Solving Problems   19

Helping Students Get "Unstuck"   21

Involving Students in Instruction   23

A Word About Word Problems   24

Questions for Discussion   26

3   Focusing on Problem-Solving Strategies   28

The Importance of Problem-Solving Strategies   28

Keys to Developing Strategies   30

Exploring the Strategies in Detail   33

Questions for Discussion   35

4   Strategy: Choose an Operation   36

   Key Words Versus Key Concepts   37
   Practice with Recognizing Key Concepts   37
   Practice with Choosing the Correct Operation   39
   Focusing on Increasingly Complex Problems   41
   A Look at Student Work   43
   Communicating About the Strategy   44
   Selecting Practice Problems   45
   Questions for Discussion   47

5   Strategy: Find a Pattern   48

   Completing and Describing Number Patterns   49
   Making Patterns Visual   50
   Working with Geometric Patterns   50
   Patterns as a Problem-Solving Strategy   51
   A Look at Student Work   51
   Communicating About the Strategy   52
   Questions for Discussion   56

6   Strategy: Make a Table   57

   Using Tables to Solve Problems   57
   Recognizing Patterns and Functions   59
   Selecting the Correct Answer   60
   Solving More Sophisticated Table Problems   60
   Using Tables to Connect to Other Math Skills   62
   Deciding When to Use a Table   62
   A Look at Student Work   63
   Communicating About the Strategy   64
   A Note About Tables   65
   Questions for Discussion   68

7   Strategy: Make an Organized List   69

   Organize and Record   69
   Laying the Foundation for More Sophisticated Skills   71
   Combinations Versus Permutations   73
   Formulas and Organized Lists   74
   A Look at Student Work   76
   Communicating About the Strategy   78
   Questions for Discussion   80

8   Strategy: Draw a Picture or Diagram   81

   A New Meaning for the Word *Picture*   82
   Simplifying Through Pictures   83
   Focusing on More Complex Problems   84
   Differentiating Instruction Through Problem Solving   85
   A Look at Student Work   86

Communicating About the Strategy   89
Questions for Discussion   91

9   Strategy: Guess, Check, and Revise   92

Beginning with a Guess   92
Revising the Guess   93
Using Guess, Check, and Revise with Equations   95
Understanding the Role of Positive Attitudes   95
Using Combined Strategies   95
Building the Foundation for More Advanced Skills   96
A Look at Student Work   96
Communicating About the Strategy   99
Questions for Discussion   100

10   Strategy: Use Logical Reasoning   101

The Role of Inferencing   102
Using a Logic Matrix   102
Using a List to Organize Clues   104
Using a Venn Diagram to Organize Ideas   105
A Look at Student Work   106
Communicating About the Strategy   108
Questions for Discussion   110

11   Strategy: Work Backward   111

Recognizing Familiar Problems   112
Increasing the Complexity of Problems   113
Working Backward with Equations   114
A Look at Student Work   115
Communicating About the Strategy   116
Questions for Discussion   119

12   Real-World Problem Solving   120

Creating Meaningful Real-World Tasks   120
Applying Classroom Skills to Meaningful Tasks   122
Utilizing the Messiness of Real-World Data   123
Discovering a World of Real Data   124
Reaping the Benefit of Real-World Activities   128
Questions for Discussion   130

13   Assessing Problem Solving   131

The Role of Ongoing Assessment   131
The Value of Observations   133
The Value of Interviews   133
The Value of Rubrics in Assessment   134
A Holistic Rubric for Problem Solving   134
The Role of Rubrics in Improvement   137
Analytic Rubrics for Assessing Specific Skills   137

Self-Reflections on Problem Solving   141
Varied Assessment   142
Questions for Discussion   143

14   Problem Solving Across the Content Standards   144

Problem Solving About Number and Operations   145
Problem Solving About Algebra   148
Problem Solving About Measurement   151
Problem Solving About Geometry   154
Problem Solving About Data and Probability   158
Linking Problem Solving and Math Content   161
Questions for Discussion   162

Conclusion: Accepting the Challenge   163
Resources to Support Teachers   169
References   173
About the CD-ROM   177

On the CD-ROM

A Guide to the CD-ROM
A Word About the CD Student Activities
Student Activities
Choose an Operation Practice Problems (12)
Find a Pattern Practice Problems (9)
Make a Table Practice Problems (10)
Make an Organized List Practice Problems (10)
Draw a Picture Practice Problems (8)
Guess, Check, and Revise Practice Problems (8)
Use Logical Reasoning Practice Problems (8)
Work Backward Practice Problems (8)
Problem-Solving Toolkit
Problem-Solving Checklists/Worksheets (8)
Pinch Cards (2)
Strategy Icons (2)
Strategy Bookmark (1)
Assessment Tools (3)
Observation Checklist (1)
Hundred Charts (2)
Car Template (1)
Candy Bag Template (1)
Cooperative Problem-Solving Cards (13)
Shape Template (1)
Real-World Problem-Solving Resources (4)
Parent Letter (1)
Problem Solving Across the Content Standards Student
Activity Pages (12)

In order to be effective mathematicians, students need to develop understanding of critical math content. They need to understand number and operations, algebra, measurement, geometry, and data analysis and probability. Through continued study of these content domains, students gain a comprehensive understanding of mathematics as a subject with varied and interconnected concepts. As math teachers, we attempt to provide students with exposure to, exploration in, and reflection about the many skills and concepts that make up the study of mathematics.

Even with a deep understanding of math content, however, students may lack important skills that can assist them in their development as effective mathematicians. Along with content knowledge, students need an understanding of the processes used by mathematicians. They must learn to problem solve, communicate their ideas, reason through math situations, prove their conjectures, make connections between and among math concepts, and represent their mathematical thinking. Development of content alone does not provide students with the means to explore, express, or apply that content. As we strive to develop effective mathematicians, we are challenged to develop both students' content understanding and process skills.

The National Council of Teachers of Mathematics (2000) has outlined critical content and process standards in its *Principles and Standards for School Mathematics* document. These standards have become the road map for the development of textbooks, curriculum materials, and student assessments. These standards have provided a framework for thinking about what needs to be taught in math classrooms and how various skills and concepts can be blended together to create a seamless math curriculum. The first five standards outline content standards and expectations related to number and operations, algebra, geometry, measurement, and data analysis and probability. The second five standards outline the process goals of problem solving, reasoning and proof, communication, connections, and representations. A strong understanding of these standards empowers teachers to identify and select activities within their curricula to produce powerful learning. The standards provide a vision for what teachers hope their students will achieve.

This book is a part of a vital series designed to assist teachers in understanding the NCTM Process Standards and the ways in which they impact and guide student learning. An additional goal of this series is to provide practical ideas to support teachers as they ensure that the acquisition of process skills has a critical place in their math instruction. Through this series, teachers will gain an understanding of each process standard as well as gather ideas for bringing that standard to life within their math classrooms. It offers practical ideas for lesson development, implementation, and assessment that work with any curriculum. Each book in the series focuses on a critical process skill in a highlighted grade band and all books are designed to encourage reflection about teaching and learning. The series also highlights the interconnected nature of the process and content standards by showing correlations between them and showcasing activities that address multiple standards.

Students who develop an understanding of content skills and cultivate the process skills that allow them to apply that content understanding become effective mathematicians. Our goal as teachers is to support and guide students as they develop both their content knowledge and their process skills, so they are able to continue to expand and refine their understanding of mathematics. This series is a guide for math educators who aspire to teach students more than math content. It is a guide to assist teachers in understanding and teaching the critical processes through which students learn and make sense of mathematics.

Susan O'Connell
Series Editor

The teaching of math problem solving can be exasperating, overwhelming, exhilarating, and gratifying, all at the same time. Each student has different strengths and weaknesses and our goal is to find ways to support and challenge each one of them. There is always more to learn about teaching problem solving!

My initial edition of this book delved into helping students understand the foundations of problem solving, the thinking skills or strategies that help them organize their thinking and work toward solutions. While those remain vital components of this second edition, the focus has expanded to encompass the broader scope of problem solving as an essential process for learning mathematics and to highlight its connections to critical math content. It has been expanded to highlight and illustrate the critical nature of the NCTM problem-solving standard.

This book is a part of an exciting new series and I would like to extend my gratitude to my colleagues in this project: Honi Bamberger, Bonnie Ennis, Brenda Hammond, Chris Oberdorf, Josie Robles, Karren Schultz-Ferrell, and Kim Witeck. I am honored to be a part of this amazing author team. The depth of their thinking, as well as the quality of their writing, has made this an exciting project and a great learning experience.

I am always excited to spend time in classrooms and want to thank the teachers and students who graciously welcomed me into their classes. It was a pleasure posing problems, hearing the student discussions, and seeing the excitement generated by the problem-solving experiences. Thanks to the following students who contributed work samples or allowed their photographs to be included in this book: Kari Adlington, Catherine Blackwood, Sarah Kate Blodgett, Jared Brown, Andrew Carbaugh, Jordan Crisler, Whitney Collins, Abi Daniel, Jacob Evans, Myea Freedman, Keegan Girouard, Jada Grey, David Greer, Emily Hall, Alexis Harder, Aaron Harten, Ben Hazel, Julie Hetrick, Julia Hiep, Joseph Hiep, Elyse Hoy, Leslie Joy, Luke Lambert, Aaron Lair, Rachel Lair, Jessica Lietz, Lindsay Littlejohn, Kaitlin McClure, Emil Mentz, Megan Merkel, Eryn Morgan, Colleen Morley, Megan Morley, Deara Moten, Lisa Murray, Haley Nalley, Victor Ojo, Toyin Orunja, Marcus Patterson, Susan Pinson, John

Quinn, Reema Saleous, Hannah Sanders, Marcela Sanidad, Chloe Schumacher, Justin Sosebee, Jeffrey Stephens, Elaine Toon, Hollis Van Fossen, and Katya Wellington.

And it was a pleasure to collaborate with many outstanding teachers as I gathered ideas and insights for this book. Special thanks to these teachers who shared student work samples or allowed me to work side-by-side with them in their classrooms: Jessica Beamon, Karen Coats, LaRenda Peterson, Peggy Price, Mike Purdy, Nancy Sawa, Alicia Whitehead, and Doug Wooton. A special thanks to Pam Landry, principal of Rockledge Elementary School in Bowie, Maryland, and Linda Bayne, principal of Sugar Grove Elementary School in Greenwood, Indiana, for allowing me to work with their outstanding teachers and students.

Delving into the NCTM process standards has been an exciting project. Special thanks to Emily Birch, my Heinemann editor, for her vision of this project. From our first discussions, she has been open to new ideas, excited about even the smallest details, and ready to guide and assist with all aspects of the project. She has embraced our ideas, enhanced our writing, and encouraged us throughout the project.

Most especially, I would like to thank my husband Pat, and my children Brendan and Katie. I am forever grateful for their support.

Problem-Solving Standard

Instructional programs from prekindergarten through grade 12 should enable all students to—

- build new mathematical knowledge through problem solving;

- solve problems that arise in mathematics and in other contexts;

- apply and adapt a variety of appropriate strategies to solve problems;

- monitor and reflect on the process of mathematical problem solving.

Reasoning and Proof Standard

Instructional programs from prekindergarten through grade 12 should enable all students to—

- recognize reasoning and proof as fundamental aspects of mathematics;

- make and investigate mathematical conjectures;

- develop and evaluate mathematical arguments and proofs;

- select and use various types of reasoning and methods of proof.

---

* Standards are listed with the permission of the National Council of Teachers of Mathematics (NCTM). NCTM does not endorse the content or validity of these alignments.

Communication Standard

Instructional programs from prekindergarten through grade 12 should enable all students to—

- organize and consolidate their mathematical thinking through communication;
- communicate their mathematical thinking coherently and clearly to peers, teachers, and others;
- analyze and evaluate the mathematical thinking and strategies of others;
- use the language of mathematics to express mathematical ideas precisely.

Connections Standards

Instructional programs from prekindergarten through grade 12 should enable all students to—

- recognize and use connections among mathematical ideas;
- understand how mathematical ideas interconnect and build on one another to produce a coherent whole;
- recognize and apply mathematics in contexts outside of mathematics.

Representation Standard

Instructional programs from prekindergarten through grade 12 should enable all students to—

- create and use representations to organize, record, and communicate mathematical ideas;
- select, apply, and translate among mathematical representations to solve problems;
- use representations to model and interpret physical, social, and mathematical phenomena.

NUMBER AND OPERATIONS

	Expectations
Instructional programs from prekindergarten through grade 12 should enable all students to—	**In grades 3–5 all students should—**
understand numbers, ways of representing numbers, relationships among numbers, and number systems	• understand the place-value structure of the base-ten number system and be able to represent and compare whole numbers and decimals; • recognize equivalent representations for the same number and generate them by decomposing and composing numbers; • develop understanding of fractions as parts of unit wholes, as parts of a collection, as locations on number lines, and as divisions of whole numbers; • use models, benchmarks, and equivalent forms to judge the size of fractions; • recognize and generate equivalent forms of commonly used fractions, decimals, and percents; • explore numbers less than 0 by extending the number line and through familiar applications; • describe classes of numbers according to characteristics such as the nature of their factors.
understand meanings of operations and how they relate to one another	• understand various meanings of multiplication and division; • understand the effects of multiplying and dividing whole numbers; • identify and use relationships between operations, such as division as the inverse of multiplication, to solve problems; • understand and use properties of operations, such as the distributivity of multiplication over addition.

	Expectations
Instructional programs from prekindergarten through grade 12 should enable all students to—	**In grades 3–5 all students should—**
compute fluently and make reasonable estimates	• develop fluency with basic number combinations for multiplication and division and use these combinations to mentally compute related problems, such as 30×50; • develop fluency in adding, subtracting, multiplying, and dividing whole numbers; • develop and use strategies to estimate the results of whole-number computations and to judge the reasonableness of such results; • develop and use strategies to estimate computations involving fractions and decimals in situations relevant to students' experience; • use visual models, benchmarks, and equivalent forms to add and subtract commonly used fractions and decimals; • select appropriate methods and tools for computing with whole numbers from among mental computation, estimation, calculators, and paper and pencil according to the context and nature of the computation and use the selected method or tools.

ALGEBRA

	Expectations
Instructional programs from prekindergarten through grade 12 should enable all students to—	**In grades 3–5 all students should—**
understand patterns, relations, and functions	• describe, extend, and make generalizations about geometric and numeric patterns; • represent and analyze patterns and functions, using words, tables, and graphs.

	Expectations
Instructional programs from prekindergarten through grade 12 should enable all students to—	**In grades 3–5 all students should—**
represent and analyze mathematical situations and structures using algebraic symbols	• identify such properties as commutativity, associativity, and distributivity and use them to compute with whole numbers; • represent the idea of a variable as an unknown quantity using a letter or a symbol; • express mathematical relationships using equations.
use mathematical models to represent and understand quantitative relationships	• model problem situations with objects and use representations such as graphs, tables, and equations to draw conclusions.
analyze change in various contexts	• investigate how a change in one variable relates to a change in a second variable; • identify and describe situations with constant or varying rates of change and compare them.

GEOMETRY

	Expectations
Instructional programs from prekindergarten through grade 12 should enable all students to—	**In grades 3–5 all students should—**
analyze characteristics and properties of two- and three-dimensional geometric shapes and develop mathematical arguments about geometric relationships	• identify, compare, and analyze attributes of two- and three-dimensional shapes and develop vocabulary to describe the attributes; • classify two- and three-dimensional shapes according to their properties and develop definitions of classes of shapes such as triangles and pyramids; • investigate, describe, and reason about the results of subdividing, combining, and transforming shapes; • explore congruence and similarity;

	Expectations
Instructional programs from prekindergarten through grade 12 should enable all students to—	**In grades 3–5 all students should—**
	• make and test conjectures about geometric properties and relationships and develop logical arguments to justify conclusions.
specify locations and describe spatial relationships using coordinate geometry and other representational systems	• describe location and movement using common language and geometric vocabulary;
	• make and use coordinate systems to specify locations and to describe paths;
	• find the distance between points along horizontal and vertical lines of a coordinate system.
apply transformations and use symmetry to analyze mathematical situations	• predict and describe the results of sliding, flipping, and turning two-dimensional shapes;
	• describe a motion or a series of motions that will show that two shapes are congruent;
	• identify and describe line and rotational symmetry in two- and three-dimensional shapes and designs.
use visualization, spatial reasoning, and geometric modeling to solve problems	• build and draw geometric objects;
	• create and describe mental images of objects, patterns, and paths;
	• identify and build a three-dimensional object from two-dimensional representations of that object;
	• identify and draw a two-dimensional representation of a three-dimensional object;
	• use geometric models to solve problems in other areas of mathematics, such as number and measurement;
	• recognize geometric ideas and relationships and apply them to other disciplines and to problems that arise in the classroom or in everyday life.

MEASUREMENT

Instructional programs from prekindergarten through grade 12 should enable all students to—	Expectations
	In grades 3–5 all students should—
understand measurable attributes of objects and the units, systems, and processes of measurement	• understand such attributes as length, area, weight, volume, and size of angle and select the appropriate type of unit for measuring each attribute; • understand the need for measuring with standard units and become familiar with standard units in the customary and metric systems; • carry out simple unit conversions, such as from centimeters to meters, within a system of measurement; • understand that measurements are approximations and how differences in units affect precision; • explore what happens to measurements of a two-dimensional shape such as its perimeter and area when the shape is changed in some way.
apply appropriate techniques, tools, and formulas to determine measurements	• develop strategies for estimating the perimeters, areas, and volumes of irregular shapes; • select and apply appropriate standard units and tools to measure length, area, volume, weight, time, temperature, and the size of angles; • select and use benchmarks to estimate measurements; • develop, understand, and use formulas to find the area of rectangles and related triangles and parallelograms; • develop strategies to determine the surface areas and volumes of rectangular solids.

Instructional programs from prekindergarten through grade 12 should enable all students to—	Expectations
	In grades 3–5 all students should—
formulate questions that can be addressed with data and collect, organize, and display relevant data to answer them	• design investigations to address a question and consider how data-collection methods affect the nature of the data set; • collect data using observations, surveys, and experiments; • represent data using tables and graphs such as line plots, bar graphs, and line graphs; • recognize the differences in representing categorical and numerical data.
select and use appropriate statistical methods to analyze data	• describe the shape and important features of a set of data and compare related data sets, with an emphasis on how the data are distributed; • use measures of center, focusing on the median, and understand what each does and does not indicate about the data set; • compare different representations of the same data and evaluate how well each representation shows important aspects of the data.
develop and evaluate inferences and predictions that are based on data	• propose and justify conclusions and predictions that are based on data and design studies to further investigate the conclusions or predictions.
understand and apply basic concepts of probability	• describe events as likely or unlikely and discuss the degree of likelihood using such words as *certain, equally likely,* and *impossible*; • predict the probability of outcomes of simple experiments and test the predictions; • understand that the measure of the likelihood of an event can be represented by a number from 0 to 1.

The Problem-Solving Standard

Solving problems is not only a goal of learning mathematics but also a major means of doing so.

—National Council of Teachers of Mathematics,
Principles and Standards for School Mathematics

Why Focus on Problem Solving?

Traditionally, problem solving was viewed as a distinct topic, introduced to students after they had mastered basic skills. In today's classrooms, however, problem solving is recognized as the central focus of mathematics instruction. The ability to solve problems is the ultimate goal of mathematics. It is why we teach students to add, subtract, multiply, and divide. It is why we teach them to work with fractions, decimals, measurement, and geometry. Our goal is not for students to perform isolated computations, but rather to be able to apply their varied math skills to solve problems. But problem solving is more than just a goal of learning mathematics, it is also a critical process, woven across the entire mathematics curriculum, through which students are able to explore and understand mathematics (NCTM 2000, 52). Through problem-solving experiences, students learn to challenge their thinking about data and probability, test their ideas about number and operations, apply their skills in geometry and measurement, and evaluate their understandings of algebra. Through problem-solving tasks, students develop an understanding of math content and ultimately use that content understanding to find solutions to problems. Problem solving is both the process by which students explore mathematics and the goal of learning mathematics.

1

One objective of problem-solving instruction is to enable students to use their repertoire of math skills to solve problems. But it takes more than isolated math skills to be an effective problem solver. It also takes a variety of thinking skills that allow students to organize ideas, select appropriate strategies, and determine the reasonableness of solutions. It takes an understanding of how to use and adapt strategies dependent on the problem situation. And it takes an ability to reflect on how we solve problems to help us better understand our own thought processes and identify why we select and apply various strategies.

While in the past, problem solving may have been viewed as an isolated assignment (e.g., a list of word problems), problem solving today has an integrated role in the math classroom. Teachers begin lessons by posing a problem, then skills and strategies are developed throughout the lesson as the problem is explored, and those newly acquired skills allow students to successfully find a solution. Problem solving becomes both the starting point and the ending point to well-balanced mathematics lessons. Developing students' computational skills is important, but teaching those skills in a problem-solving context ensures that students not only understand the skill but see the meaningfulness of learning the skill and understand how to apply it to real-world situations. "Problem solving is the process by which students experience the power and usefulness of mathematics in the world around them" (NCTM 1989, 75).

What Is the Problem-Solving Process Standard?

The National Council of Teachers of Mathematics (NCTM) has developed standards in order to support and guide teachers as they develop classroom lessons and create activities to build their students' mathematical understandings. Some of those standards delineate the content to be addressed in the math classroom, while other standards address the processes by which students explore and use mathematics. Problem solving is a critical math process and the components of the NCTM Problem Solving Process Standard reflect its complex nature. Instructional programs (NCTM 2000, 52) should enable students to

- build new mathematical knowledge through problem solving;

- solve problems that arise in mathematics and in other contexts;

- apply and adapt a variety of appropriate strategies to solve problems;

- monitor and reflect on the process of mathematical problem solving.

Throughout this book, we explore ways to assist students in building new math knowledge through problem-solving tasks. Highlighted problem-solving activities may be presented in math contexts as well as real-world contexts. We explore, in depth, the various problem-solving strategies that support students in finding solutions, and we identify techniques for helping students reflect and monitor their problem solving. We will dive into the NCTM process standard of problem solving in order to better understand it and find ways to bring it to life within our classrooms.

Creating Effective Problem Solvers

In my early experiences with teaching problem solving, I began much like my own teachers had, assigning problems to students and expecting them to be able to solve the problems on their own. I quickly recognized my students' anxiety and frustration. I soon learned that assigning problems and then correcting those problems did not create successful problem solvers. I began to break down the skills needed to solve problems and find opportunities to guide my students in developing some specific strategies to help them organize their thinking. Through a combination of modeling, providing opportunities for exploration, facilitating discussions about thinking, and prompting students to reflect on their experiences, I observed the continued efficiency with which my students solved problems. The more they explored and analyzed problem-solving strategies, the more successful they became. Surprisingly, not just the most capable of my students showed progress, but all of them did. As I demonstrated various strategies to attack problems and began to let my students see math problems through visual and hands-on demonstrations, their skills improved. And my skills improved, too! The more comfortable I became at teaching problem solving, the more confident I became about my ability to help my students understand a process that had once seemed so complicated and abstract.

With an understanding of the problem-solving process and a repertoire of strategies to assist our students in dealing with problem situations, our anxiety and frustration lessen and our enthusiasm and confidence grow. Not all students can become effective problem solvers on their own, but with the help of a confident and capable teacher, all students can significantly improve their problem-solving abilities.

Developing Skills and Attitudes

Developing students' problem-solving abilities is a challenging and complex task. It requires attention to the building of mathematical skills and thinking processes as well as attention to the development of positive attitudes toward problem solving. Both skills and attitudes must be strengthened to produce truly effective problem solvers.

Problem solving is a process, requiring students to follow a series of steps to find a solution. Although some students may intuitively follow a process, many students need to be taught how to proceed to reach a solution. Another important goal in teaching students to solve problems is assisting them in developing strategies or plans for solving problems. While choosing a mathematical operation—addition, subtraction, multiplication, or division—is frequently the way to solve a problem, alternate strategies are often needed. Helping students learn strategies such as drawing pictures, finding patterns, making tables, making lists, guessing and checking, working backward, or using logical reasoning gives students a wide variety of strategies to employ during problem solving. Problem solving requires this knowledge of strategies as well as the ability to determine when each strategy would be best used. The more our students practice these strategies, the more confident they become in their ability to solve problems and apply mathematics in meaningful ways.

The development of a positive attitude toward problem solving is crucial to student success. As teachers, we are instrumental in helping our students develop the attitudes needed to become successful problem solvers.

Problem solving requires patience.

It is not always possible to find a quick answer and quick answers are often incorrect. Problem solving is not judged on speed but on the reasonableness of the final solution.

Problem solving requires persistence.

Students may need to try several strategies before finding one that will work. Students must have confidence that they can find a solution, even if it is not immediately apparent.

Problem solving requires risk taking.

Students need to be willing to try their "hunches," hoping that they may lead to a solution. Students must feel comfortable making mistakes, as problem solving is a process filled with mistakes that often lead to solutions.

Problem solving requires cooperation.

Students must often be willing to share ideas, build on one another's thoughts, and work together to find a solution.

Students become successful problem solvers when they are instructed in a climate that rewards patience, persistence, risk taking, and cooperation. As teachers, we have a critical role in establishing a positive climate for problem-solving instruction.

How This Book Will Help You

This book is designed to help you better understand the NCTM problem-solving standard. It explores problem solving as both a process through which students learn mathematics and a skill that enables them to apply the mathematics they have learned. The mathematical goals of students in grades 3–5 are specifically addressed and practical ideas for helping students become effective problem solvers are shared.

This book presents ideas for developing a problem-centered approach to teaching mathematics within your classroom. We will see how problem solving can set a context for learning math skills, can excite and engage students, and can help students discover insights and better understand math ideas. We explore ways in which problem solving enriches our math classrooms and nurtures enthusiasm, curiosity, and insight.

Within this book you will find a variety of ideas to help you better understand the problem-solving process, as well as specific strategies including Choose an Operation; Find a Pattern; Make a Table; Make an Organized List; Draw a Picture or Diagram; Guess, Check, and Revise; Use Logical Reasoning; and Work Backward. These strategies help students organize their thinking, figure out ways to approach and simplify problems, and ultimately find their way to solutions. We explore practical ways to support our students as they develop these thinking skills, knowing that the groundwork for each strategy is laid in the primary grades, but that students in grades 3–5 refine their use of these strategies and engage in tasks requiring a more sophisticated understanding. As we investigate a variety of problem-solving strategies, we delve into their underlying skills in order to unearth the complexity and importance of each strategy. A variety of activities that are appropriate for students in grades 3–5 are shared for each strategy. Specific grade levels are not indicated on each activity, as problem-solving skills do not develop by grade level, but rather depend on students' prior knowledge and previous exposure to each strategy. Teacher tips are shared highlighting important points to emphasize when working with students. Examples of student work are presented for each strategy, including samples of students' communication about their problem solving. The work samples illustrate the progression of problem-solving skills, and the writing samples offer a glimpse into students' thinking as their skills develop.

Once we have explored the problem-solving standard in depth, you will see how it connects to the math content standards in the chapter Problem Solving Across the Content Standards. Through sample classroom activities, we explore the interconnectedness of the content and process standards. We discuss sample problem-solving tasks that blend with grades 3 through 5 content in number and operations, algebra, geometry, measurement, and data and probability. Student work is shared to illustrate these lessons and you will be asked to reflect on the combined teaching of math content and the problem-solving process.

In later chapters we discuss the assessment of problem solving including the use of rubrics to assess students' skills. We also explore real-world problem-solving tasks that challenge students to move beyond the context of math and apply their skills to everyday situations. These tasks motivate and engage students and demonstrate the meaningfulness of the mathematics they are learning. Ideas for using real-world data and materials are presented.

While this book is designed to help you better understand the NCTM Problem Solving Standard and to provide you with practical ideas and classroom activities related to the standard, it is also intended to stimulate thought about teaching and learning. Following each chapter, several questions prompt you to reflect on the content of the chapter whether alone or with a group of your colleagues. Taking a moment to reflect on the ideas presented, and relating them to your teaching experiences and your observations of your students, will help you better process the ideas and apply them to your students' specific needs.

A very important component of this book is the inclusion of the practical resources needed to implement the ideas explored throughout the chapters. The accompanying CD is filled with a variety of teacher-ready materials to help you implement a problem-solving program in your school or classroom. Checklists, evaluation forms, scoring keys, and icons are all available as well as a variety of practice problems for your students. The practice problems range from simple to complex. Select those activities that suit your students' level of expertise, and continue to challenge your students with more sophisticated thinking as their skills improve. And many of the activities and resources on the CD can be easily modified to suit your students' specific needs. Change the data to make it less or more challenging, or insert familiar names and places to engage and motivate your students as they explore the problem activities.

This book was developed as a result of my readings about problem-solving theory, my reflection on current practices, and my observations on the progress of students in varied classroom settings. As a result of both research and practice, I have adapted and modified some common problem-solving techniques, developed some new activities to support problem-solving instruction, and highlighted resources and activities that are particularly effective for students in grades 3–5. It is hoped that this book will enhance your understanding of the problem-solving standard and provide you with insights and practical ideas to develop your students' problem-solving skills. When we, as teachers, better understand the complexity and importance of problem solving, we are better able to identify, select, and design meaningful tasks for our students. It is hoped that the varied instructional practices highlighted in this book will assist you in developing your students' skills and expanding your own understandings. Most certainly, as we reflect on and develop our teaching skills, our students' problem-solving skills will increase as well.

Questions for Discussion

1. Were you taught how to solve math problems or just assigned problems to solve? How did you feel about math problem solving when you were a student in the math classroom? In what ways do your past experiences and attitudes about problem solving impact your teaching of problem solving?

2. If students show competence with computational skills but lack problem-solving skills, how might it effect their math achievement? What possible problems might they experience?

3. What attitudes are essential to be an effective problem solver? How might you support students in developing these attitudes?

4. What skills are essential to be an effective problem solver? How might you help your students acquire those skills?

CHAPTER 1

Building Math Understanding Through Problem Solving

A problem-centered approach to teaching mathematics uses interesting and well-selected problems to launch mathematical lessons and engage students. In this way, new ideas, techniques, and mathematical relationships emerge and become the focus of discussion.

—National Council of Teachers of Mathematics,
Principles and Standards for School Mathematics

"Math was boring!" is a comment heard from many adults remembering endless worksheets and rote textbook assignments. For many of us, math was a process of memorizing facts and procedures and plugging numbers into formulas. There was nothing memorable or exciting about activities in our math classrooms. We completed tasks without even thinking about the meaning of what we were doing. We were bored by the process, hazy in our understanding of the concepts, and unsure of how to apply the skills to problem situations. We want our students to have a different math experience. We want them to be actively engaged in our lessons, excited to explore math ideas, and challenged to reason and problem solve about mathematics. We need more than worksheets to accomplish that!

In today's classrooms, our goal is to help our students use their math knowledge to solve problems rather than to mechanically perform computations. Problem solving is both a goal and a vehicle for our students. Our goal is for them to apply their understanding of math concepts and skills to find solutions to the varied problems they might face, and the problem-solving experiences are the vehicle through which our students are able to explore, discuss, and develop a variety of math skills. We want our students to learn *about* problem solving as well as learn *through* problem solving. We want more for our students than simply to memorize a series of math skills and concepts. Recent research and professional discussions support the power of problem-centered instruction (Hiebert et al., 1997; Lester and Charles, 2003; Van de Walle and Lovin, 2006). We have recognized its value in helping students better understand important math ideas. Problem-centered instruction is a significant tool for helping students examine, predict, observe, discover, and ultimately use mathematics.

Teaching Math Through Problems

Lecture, combined with drill and practice, have been the typical teaching scenario in math classrooms. Our teachers identified key ideas and told us what we needed to know, and then asked us to practice the skills until we had committed them to memory. Students with strong rote skills were able to effectively memorize facts and ideas, often realizing later that they did not understand the processes they had memorized. Students with poor rote skills struggled with memorizing ideas that had no meaning to them and often became frustrated and disenchanted with mathematics. In recent years we have recognized that problem-solving tasks motivate and engage students in a way that lecture and drill-and-practice tasks are unable to do. Students are naturally inquisitive. They like to explore, investigate, and hypothesize. They become excited and energized by new problems. And problem-solving tasks provide our students with opportunities to explore and understand the formulas and algorithms that we were asked to simply memorize. Rather than classrooms in which students are bored with rote facts and formulas, we are striving for classrooms in which our students are excited about math, discover math ideas, and continually build on their math knowledge. Through problem-solving tasks, we are able to transform our classrooms from lecture halls to laboratories.

In problem-centered instruction, rather than telling students key math ideas, problems are posed to engage students in exploration and promote thinking about the important mathematical concepts. Students explore problems with partners or groups and are guided in that exploration by the teacher. Students are actively engaged in learning. They are asked to communicate their ideas, share their insights, apply their previously learned knowledge to new situations, reflect on their experiences, and ultimately discover new math ideas. Through problem tasks, new knowledge is built on existing knowledge. In problem-based instruction, the process of learning is as important as the content being learned. Students are learning new ideas but are also learning "how" to learn new ideas.

A Look at Problem-Centered Instruction

In problem-centered instruction, problems are posed that become a starting point for student learning. The problem investigation sets the context through which students are challenged to use their already acquired skills to develop new understandings. As students look at a concept or skill in a problem context, they often formulate questions, test ideas, and ultimately grow to better understand the concept. When exploring the concept of area, students might be challenged to find the area of a triangle. Rather than being told the formula, they work together to use their understandings about finding the area of a square, their spatial sense, and their knowledge of operations to figure out a way to find the unknown area. As they dive into the task, they begin to better understand the concept of area. Fifth graders shared their strategies for finding the area of a triangle with these insights:

> *"You could just put two triangles together and get a square so it is half of the area of the square."*

> *"The triangle section of the figure is half the area of the square section because if you doubled it you would have the square. So you could just find the area as if it was a square and find half of that."*

Through their own investigations, discussions, and insights, these students were able to process the concept of area and determine a way to calculate the area of a triangle. Now, even before it appears in their textbooks, they have begun to discover the formula for finding the area of a triangle and it makes sense to them! Through active involvement in exploring problem situations, students are challenged to begin with what they know about math and through the exploration, build on that understanding to create new and more refined understandings.

Problem-solving tasks require the application of math skills. During problem-solving tasks, students are challenged to move beyond simply solving algorithms. Students are challenged to determine how to solve a problem and see real examples of the usefulness of math skills. Rather than adding fractions on worksheets, students see the application of adding fractions as they figure out how many pizzas they will need if John eats $\frac{1}{2}$ pizza, Alex eats $\frac{1}{3}$ pizza, and Jamie eats $\frac{1}{4}$ pizza. Would one pizza be enough? Would two pizzas be too much? The fractions become more than just numbers, they now represent a real problem and the skill of adding fractions becomes relevant.

Selecting Meaningful Tasks

Problem-based instruction, however, is more than simply posing a problem and asking students to solve it. In problem-centered instruction, teachers are challenged to select appropriate tasks, guide students as they engage in the tasks, and assess their understanding of the mathematics. These essential teacher responsibilities impact the success of the problem-solving activity.

Selecting tasks that lead students to important math learning is fundamental. We may want students to discover a formula, learn to organize information for analysis, or apply computational skills or conceptual understanding to real or mathematical situations. Good problems set the stage for our students to explore and discover significant math ideas. If selected carefully, problem-solving tasks can motivate and engage students in learning math, can illustrate the application of math skills, can support students in the development of new math understanding, and can provide assessment of students' strengths and weaknesses. Meaningful tasks do not need to be lengthy and can be set in a math context or a real-world context, but they need to address important math skills and promote thought about those skills. A look at content standards and indicators will provide you with ideas of critical skills.

Problem-solving tasks can set a context for the learning of a skill or can challenge students to apply already learned skills. Teachers might introduce students to equivalent fractions by asking them to find all of the different ways they could make $\frac{1}{2}$ using a variety of fractional pieces. As they measure and explore, they begin to find that two of the $\frac{1}{4}$ pieces are the same as $\frac{1}{2}$ or that three of the $\frac{1}{6}$ pieces would work, too. Students find solutions using manipulatives prior to their understanding of equivalent fractions, and the exploration paves the way for better understanding of the representations $\frac{1}{2}, \frac{2}{4}, \frac{3}{6} \ldots$.

Since mathematics is about both content and process, problem-solving activities can lead students to insights about either. Content insights might include discoveries about the relationship between area and perimeter as students explore the number of students who can sit around ten tables. While the area (ten square units) does not change, the configuration of the tables changes the perimeters. Discoveries about flips, slides, and turns emerge as students attempt to create figures with tangram pieces. While it may appear that there is no way to create a parallelogram using a square and two small triangles, a flip or a turn allows students to complete the task. In addition, problem tasks support students' development of process skills including ways to represent information, organize information, observe data, and draw conclusions. As students work to find all of the possible combinations when they roll two number cubes (dice) in a probability exploration, they use ways to organize the data to be sure they have not missed any combinations and find ways to record the data so they can draw conclusions about their findings. Through the selection of appropriate problems, students can be challenged to develop and refine their thinking about math content and processes.

The Role of Communication

Guiding students as they explore problems is critical to the success of problem-centered instruction. Support comes in many shapes and sizes. As we observe students during problem tasks, we look for cues to let us know when support or encouragement is needed as frustration sets in or when additional challenges are appropriate. Through questioning to guide their thinking or stimulate ideas or through class debriefing to highlight discoveries, teachers play an active role in ensuring that students are thinking as they work and are learning from the experience.

When we observe students solving problems, we often notice students who are intuitively able to apply strategies as they work through a problem. Others, however, appear to be perplexed as to how to tackle the problem, unable to organize the data in a way that will help them understand it. A goal during problem-solving tasks is to glean insights from those who are using appropriate strategies, help some students identify what they are intuitively doing, and help others gain insight into reasonable approaches for problem-solving tasks. Language in the math classroom is a key for helping students recognize their own and each other's thinking. It makes thinking visible within the classroom.

Through teacher talk, we introduce the task, clarify the question, and guide students in the investigation. After posing the problem, we might clarify it using some examples to help students understand their task. As students work together to solve problems, we ask questions to stimulate thought or redirect efforts. Our words are influential in helping students discover ideas.

Student talk is also a critical component of problem-based instruction. Students should work with partners or groups to foster math talk about their thinking. Through partner and group work we allow students to struggle with ideas and build on each other's insights or allow a natural form of tutoring to occur as some students explain their insights to others. Through facilitating class discussions we allow students to express their thoughts and insights and allow others to hear their ideas and meld them into their own. Through presentations to share their solutions and approaches, we allow opportunities for all students to see multiple solutions and approaches as well as to hear related ideas as they work to support their own findings.

In problem-centered instruction, the goal is not a correct answer, although we do love correct answers! The goal is to explore a task, determine a strategy to get to a solution, and learn about math along the way. Students might find varied, but equally reasonable, ways to get to a solution. Allowing students to report about their insights and share their strategies is important in extending the understanding of all students within the classroom. Even wrong answers or illogical strategies are part of the learning process in problem-based instruction. Errors often lead to insights for students and certainly help us better understand our students' thinking.

Figure 1–1 *Active engagement in problem-solving experiences helps students make sense of math.*

A Look at a Problem-Based Lesson

Students discover many key math ideas when given opportunities to problem solve and discuss their observations. In Mrs. Connor's third grade classroom, students were exploring fractions. Mrs. Connor gave each pair of students a brown fraction bar (one strip of paper with a line in the center to divide it into two equal parts) and told them that the paper represented a candy bar. She asked them to determine the fraction of the bar that they could each eat if they shared the candy bar equally. Students quickly stated that they could each eat $\frac{1}{2}$ of the bar. Mrs. Connor recorded $\frac{1}{2}$ on the blackboard and asked students to remind her what the numerator and denominator in $\frac{1}{2}$ represented. Students were able to explain that each person would get one piece (numerator) and there were two pieces (denominator) in the whole bar. Mrs. Connor then explained that she had some other candy bars that were divided in parts. The student pairs would need to decide the fraction of each candy bar that they could eat remembering that they needed to share each bar equally. She asked her students to be sure to record their solutions and to be ready to defend them. Student pairs were each given a blue fraction bar divided into fourths, a red bar divided into eighths, and a yellow bar divided into tenths. Each whole bar was the same size.

After allowing the students to work with their partners, discuss their ideas, and determine the fraction of each bar that they could eat, Mrs. Connor asked each pair to compare their answers with the pair sitting across from them and to explain to each other how they came up with their solutions. Mrs. Connor moved through the classroom to listen and observe as pairs shared and explained their solutions. Mrs. Connor then brought the whole class together for a discussion of their insights.

Most students responded that they would get $\frac{2}{4}$ of the blue bar because they would each get two of the four pieces. Mrs. Connor recorded $\frac{2}{4}$ on the board. Sherry and Thomas, however, had a different idea and contended that they would get $\frac{1}{2}$ of the bar. "Why would you get $\frac{1}{2}$?" Mrs. Connor probed. "Well, we first thought $\frac{2}{4}$, but when we lined them up next to each other we saw we each got the same amount so we each got $\frac{1}{2}$ of the bar," Sherry explained. "Yeah and the two pieces were the same size as the one piece that was half last time," chimed in Thomas. "What do you think about Sherry's and Thomas' observations?" Mrs. Connor asked the class. "It has to be $\frac{2}{4}$ because there are four pieces. That's how you write fractions." said Carrie. "They are the same size, but you say $\frac{2}{4}$," agreed Jon. After several more students shared their contentions, Mrs. Connor asked students about the red bar and the yellow bar. "It's $\frac{4}{8}$ and $\frac{5}{10}$," one student quickly responded. "But they're like $\frac{1}{2}$," said another who again noticed the similarity in the size of the candy she would get to eat. Mrs. Connor wrote $\frac{4}{8}$ and $\frac{5}{10}$ on the board. Mrs. Connor asked, "If I asked for $\frac{4}{8}$ of your candy bar, would I get more, less, or the same as if I asked for $\frac{1}{2}$ of your candy bar?" The students were quiet and Mrs. Connor asked them to discuss the idea with their partners. She then walked through the room listening for evidence of their understanding or confusion. She heard Jerome adamantly express that $\frac{4}{8}$ of his candy bar would be more than $\frac{1}{2}$ of it, while Karen was sure it would be the same. Mrs. Connor reminded the students that they could see the bars and try out their hunches with the manipulatives (fraction bars) at their desks. She also reminded them to observe the numbers that they had recorded as their solutions. "Good problem solvers are very observant," she reminded her class. Sometimes on their own, and a few times with her help, students began to convince one another that the fractions did represent the same amount of candy.

Mrs. Connor again facilitated a discussion asking students to defend their ideas. Students showed illustrations to prove that $\frac{4}{8}$ and $\frac{1}{2}$ were the same or lined-up fraction bars to make their case, and Emily blurted out, "Hey, you always have double on the bottom." "What do you mean?" Mrs. Connor probed. "The denominator is twice as much as the numerator like $\frac{5}{10}$ or $\frac{4}{8}$ just like in $\frac{1}{2}$." "That's interesting! Why do you suppose the numbers look that way?" Mrs. Connor asked students to discuss their ideas with their partners. Kelly summed up her thoughts with, "Well, if I gave you the same amount as I keep then I would have half of the number on the bottom, so half will always be that way."

Mrs. Connor walked to the overhead projector and put some colored counters on it. She played with various quantities always equaling $\frac{1}{2}$ to test their theory. She recorded each fraction on the overhead so students could observe the numerator and denominator. Mrs. Connor then asked students to work with their partners to come up with more fractions that equaled $\frac{1}{2}$ using the following denominators: 16, 20, 24, and 30. During class sharing, Jerome claimed that $\frac{20}{40}$ would work and was the same as $\frac{1}{2}$ because he would get twenty pieces and his friend would get twenty pieces and they would each have the same, half of the candy but noted that they would get "really small pieces." And Jenna shared a "trick" she found: all she needed to do was multiply each number by the same number and she could make lots of fractions that equal $\frac{1}{2}$ like you multiply each number by 2 and you get $\frac{2}{4}$ or by 5 and you get $\frac{5}{10}$ or by 20 and you get $\frac{20}{40}$. Mrs. Connor and the class tried Jenna's trick with some other numbers and each time got a fraction that was the same as $\frac{1}{2}$. Mrs. Connor then asked each group of four students to make a list of some of the things they learned—their discoveries! She listed their discoveries on the board including:

1. You can say $\frac{1}{2}$ in lots of ways.

2. If it is $\frac{1}{2}$, the numerator has to be half as much as the denominator.

3. One-half and $\frac{5}{10}$ are the same amount.

4. You could find more fractions for $\frac{1}{2}$ by multiplying both numbers by the same number and it will always be $\frac{1}{2}$.

Through the problem exploration, Mrs. Connor led her students to explore the concept of equivalent fractions. Rather than beginning with a lecture on how to create equivalent fractions by multiplying numerator and denominator by the same number, she chose to allow students to gain an understanding of the concept and in so doing also set the stage for the discovery of the computational skill. Mrs. Connor selected a problem task with significant mathematics and allowed students to explore the task and build understanding. She allowed misconceptions, knowing that they are just an expression of students' thinking, but used the misconceptions to question and prompt students to further explore the ideas. She provided many opportunities for math talk, with partners, groups, and the whole class. And she repeatedly asked students to justify their answers. By asking students to summarize their discoveries, Mrs. Connor helped students reflect on their learning and asked them to process that learning by writing a summary of their discoveries. She recorded key ideas on the board to allow all students to see, hear, and think about the key ideas that grew out of the lesson. Through task selection, thoughtful grouping, and frequent prompting and questioning, the teacher was able to lead her students to important insights about equivalent fractions in a way that engaged them, stimulated their thinking, and built new math understandings.

During this task, students were challenged to apply their current understanding of fractions to a new situation. They used what they knew to further develop their understanding of fractions. They used their observation skills of number patterns to recognize changes in the numerators and denominators, and they applied thinking skills to help them organize, record, and analyze the information. Problem-based instruction supports students with math concepts, computation, and thinking skills as it challenges them to use all of them to find and defend solutions.

Problems as a Teaching Tool

As we become more comfortable allowing students to explore problems even before some skills have been taught, we begin to recognize that students often discover many math ideas on their own. Posing problems frequently enough to allow students to explore skills, learn to apply skills, and in so doing advance their thinking, arouse their curiosity, and generate insights, is a goal of problem-centered instruction. Problems are a tool for extending our students' understanding of math.

Problem solving is both a process and a skill. It is a process, a way in which students learn about math ideas. Through problem explorations, students expand their understanding of math concepts and develop their math skills. But problem solving is also a skill to be learned by students. Through the development of some critical problem-solving strategies, which we explore in the following chapters, students can become more skillful at solving even complex math problems.

CLASSROOM-TESTED TIP

Involving All Students

For group problem-solving tasks, consider ways to organize the experience so that all students in the group become involved in the task. Assigning group jobs is a way to engage everyone in the activity. Typical jobs might include leader, reporter, checker, recorder, or materials manager. Passing out cards to each member with their job designation will remind them of their role. Be sure to explain each job so students will understand their responsibilities. Some typical job descriptions might be:

- The leader reads the problem and makes sure everyone has a chance to speak.

- The reporter shares the group solution with the class.

- The recorder writes down ideas as the group discusses the task.

- The checker double-checks the group's work when the students believe they are done.

- The materials manager gathers, distributes, or cleans up any manipulatives used by the group during the task.

Assigning jobs does not mean that students each do a part of the task, as collaboration is critical. The jobs simply organize the task to ensure that all students participate in the problem-solving experience and contribute toward the solution.

Questions for Discussion

1. How is the teacher's role different in problem-centered instruction than in the traditional drill-and-practice style of teaching math? How is the student's role different?

2. What is the role of teacher questioning in a problem-centered classroom? What is the role of student-to-student talk?

3. How can the teacher ensure that students are actually learning key ideas and concepts? How might teachers guide students to discoveries?

4. What can the teacher do to support students who are having difficulty solving problems?

CHAPTER 2

Guiding Students Through the Problem-Solving Process

The instructional goal is that students will build an increasing repertoire of strategies, approaches, and familiar problems; it is the problem-solving process that is most important, not just the answer.

—National Council of Teachers of Mathematics,
Curriculum and Evaluation Standards for School Mathematics

Teaching math concepts through a problem-centered approach provides opportunities for our students to discover and refine important math ideas. While some students may intuitively know how to approach the problem tasks, organize their thinking, and select appropriate strategies to find solutions, many others need opportunities to identify and develop their problem-solving skills. Whether we are helping our intuitive problem solvers refine their skills or helping our struggling problem solvers develop their skills, attention to the problem-solving process and key problem-solving strategies is essential.

The Problem-Solving Process

Problem solving is a multistep task. Successful problem solvers move through a series of steps toward the solution. This does not mean that every student thinks through each step in the same way, but that a process occurs within the heads of problem solvers to help them move through a problem from start to finish. Polya (2004) first identified steps in the problem-solving process, and those steps have been used, discussed, and adapted in numerous problem-solving programs and curricula. Helping students identify these steps helps them view problem solving as a series of actions that leads to the eventual solution. The more proficient our students become with the process, the more quickly and intuitively they may move through these steps; but initially, focusing our students on each step will ensure that they have considered the data, developed a logical plan of action, and carried out the plan in an accurate and reasonable way. Following is a checklist that guides students through the critical steps of the problem-solving process:

Problem-Solving Checklist

> Understand the question.
> Choose a plan.
> Try your plan.
> Check your answer.
> Reflect on what you've done.

Breaking Down the Process

Step 1: Understand the Question

This first step in the problem-solving process asks students to think about the problem and decide what they are being asked to solve. This is an important step in focusing students for the problem-solving task ahead. We have all experienced watching students labor over finding the answer to the *wrong question*. If students are uncertain what they are being asked to solve, the likelihood that they will successfully progress through the remaining steps is poor. In this initial step in the problem-solving process, students restate the problem in their own words, explaining what it is asking them to do. Students might be given written problems and asked to identify the question, either by circling the "question" part of the problem or by writing the question in their own words. They might be asked to work in pairs or groups to determine what the problem is asking them to do. Hearing each other's thoughts will strengthen their skills for understanding problems. And understanding the question leads our students to discussions about the data they believe will be useful in solving the problem.

When practicing this first step in the problem-solving process, students do not need to solve each problem that is posed to them. Isolating the skill of identifying and understanding the question and practicing that skill without moving through all of the steps of the problem-solving process helps students strengthen their skills in this area.

Step 2: Choose a Plan

In this critical step, students must decide *how* to solve the problem. Students will need to identify a plan or strategy for solving the problem. Students may recognize that the problem can be solved with one of the basic operations—addition, subtraction, multiplication, or division—or they may discover that an alternate strategy—making a list, a table, or diagram; working backward; finding a pattern; guessing and checking; or using logical reasoning—may be more effective for solving the problem. Students will need to identify the known data (the data mentioned in the problem) that will help them solve the problem and will have to determine what to do with that data to get to the solution. Students may look for key concepts to help them decide on a strategy or may relate the problem to other familiar problems in order to help them decide how to proceed. Often, more than one strategy can be used to solve a problem. Discussions at this stage will help students appreciate the different ways that problems can be solved. The more practice that students have in determining an appropriate strategy, the more skilled they will become at selecting a strategy on their own. And whenever possible, having students predict the answer, after they have determined their plan, will provide them with a benchmark later in the process as they look back to check the reasonableness of their answer.

Step 3: Try Your Plan

Now it's time for students to put the selected strategy to use. In this step, the student uses his or her strategy to attempt to find a solution. Consider allowing students to use calculators to help them focus on the problem-solving process. Often, students' anxiety or confusion regarding the calculations distracts them from the primary objective of the lesson, which relates to their problem-solving skills. When assessing students' ability to solve problems, calculators will help both you and your students focus on the problem-solving objectives. The use of calculators also reduces the amount of time needed to calculate answers and gives students more time to spend on the "thinking" part of the process. Most importantly, calculators help students recognize the significant and appropriate role of technology in assisting them in finding solutions.

At times, students may try their plans and find that those plans do not lead to a solution. This is an important realization. Students need to recognize that trying and then eliminating a strategy is okay. Finding a solution does not always happen on the first try. Recognizing that a strategy was unsuccessful and deciding on an alternate strategy are important skills in building effective problem solvers.

Step 4: Check Your Answer

Traditionally, this step has focused on checking for calculation errors. While checking for arithmetic accuracy is important, it is equally important that students recognize that checking their answers includes checking the reasonableness of the answers. If students predicted an answer before trying their plans, this is the time for them to compare their predicted and actual answers to see if they are compatible. Encourage students to ask themselves questions like, "Does this answer make sense?" "Is something not quite right here?"

Even without a prediction, students are often able to recognize when an answer does not seem reasonable. Asking students to write a summary sentence that relates their answer to the question will force them to look at the question and their answer together and will often help them detect unreasonable answers. This technique is especially helpful for those students who rush from problem to problem, doing the calculations and never looking back to check for reasonableness.

Consider the following problem:

There were 500 students at the assembly. 240 students were boys. How many girls were at the assembly?

Summary sentence: **There were 500 students at the assembly. 240 of them were boys, and 740 of them were girls.**

The realization: *"That can't be right! There were only 500 students at the assembly."*

Step 5: Reflect on What You've Done

Once the problem has been solved, it is time for students to sit back and reflect on their actions and insights throughout the process. Students might be asked to explain how they solved the problem or to justify their solution. They might be asked to share other ways of solving the problem or to reflect on what was easy or hard about the task. This step allows students to process what they've done, and it gives teachers valuable insight into students' thinking. In the teaching of problem solving, this is a critical step as it supports students in better understanding their own thinking (metacognition). It is the step in which students recognize and verbalize how they solved a problem and why they solved it in that way.

Recording Steps in Solving Problems

As with many skills that are multistep, showing students how to monitor the problem-solving process through the use of writing as a tool to organize and record their ideas will help them process and remember the steps to solving problems. Many teachers use checklists or worksheets to help students internalize the thinking process. Initially, students need to understand what is required at each step of the process. They need to see the steps modeled and they benefit from moving through each step until it becomes routine. In the early stages, completing a process checklist or worksheet like the examples on the CD will help students organize their thinking and serve to remind students of the steps in the problem-solving process. These checklists or worksheets (see Figure 2–1) support students by allowing them to process their ideas as they record them. The format of students' writing might vary, as illustrated in the varied formats on the CD, but the main components (the steps in the problem-solving process) remain consistent to help students remember important steps to consider when solving problems. Some teachers prefer worksheets on which students complete each section as they move through each step, others may prefer to offer students open-ended prompts to guide them through the steps like:

Understand the Question	I (We) need to find out . . .
	I (We) already know . . .
Make a Plan	To get the answer I (we) could . . .
	I (We) think the answer will be . . .

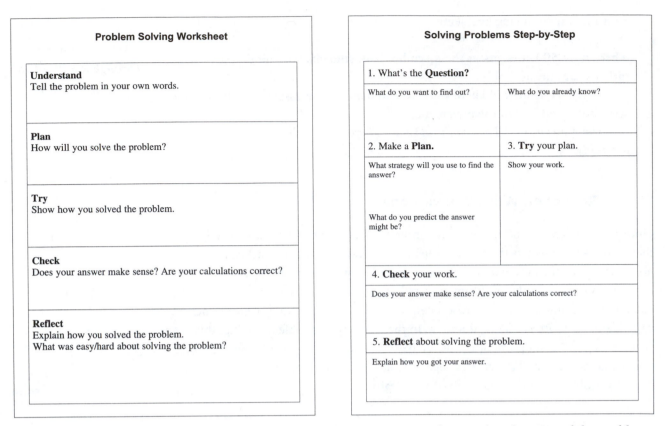

Problem Solving Worksheet

Understand
Tell the problem in your own words.

Plan
How will you solve the problem?

Try
Show how you solved the problem.

Check
Does your answer make sense? Are your calculations correct?

Reflect
Explain how you solved the problem.
What was easy/hard about solving the problem?

Solving Problems Step-by-Step

1. What's the **Question?**	
What do you want to find out?	What do you already know?

2. Make a **Plan.**	3. **Try** your plan.
What strategy will you use to find the answer?	Show your work.
What do you predict the answer might be?	

4. **Check** your work.

Does your answer make sense? Are your calculations correct?

5. **Reflect** about solving the problem.

Explain how you got your answer.

Figure 2–1 *Asking students to record their ideas helps them recognize and remember the steps of the problem-solving process.*

Try Your Plan   Here is my (our) work . . .
Check Your Work   My (Our) answer makes sense because . . .
Reflect About Solving the Problem   I (We) got my (our) answer by . . .
                                            I (We) had trouble. . . . But I (we) . . .

 Many students are familiar with K-W-L charts (What I *Know*, What I *Want* to Know, What I *Learned*) from using them to record ideas in other (nonmath) content areas. Using modified K-W-L charts, like the ones on the CD, are also an effective way for students to record their ideas as they work through the problem-solving process (see the examples in Figure 2–2). Regardless of which format you choose, these recording tools support your students as they explore the thinking process required when solving math problems.

As students become more skilled at the process, a written checklist or worksheet may no longer be needed and may even become frustrating to students who have internalized the problem-solving process and are now focusing their attentions on other problem-solving skills. Stopping at each step to record their actions may begin to distract them from solving the problem. Our knowledge of our students' abilities, gathered through constant monitoring and assessment, helps us recognize those students who will benefit from a step-by-step approach and those who will be more effective without the structured checklist.

Problem-Solving K-W-P-L

What I **Know**	What I **Want** to Find Out	What I **Plan** to Do	What I **Learned**

Figure 2–2 *Modified K-W-L charts help students organize and record their thinking during problem solving.*

Providing a checklist for selected students is a good way to address the different needs of the students in our classrooms. Students can be asked to make notes on the checklist as they proceed through the steps of the process, or the checklist can be used to stimulate discussion among partners, teams, or the entire class. The checklist might be posted in the classroom to support students during class discussions or as a resource to which they can refer during independent work. It serves to remind students of the important steps in the problem-solving process.

Helping Students Get "Unstuck"

Students often become stuck when attempting to solve problems. When solutions are not immediately apparent, students can become frustrated and give up. Helping them learn ways to get themselves "unstuck" is an important lesson in their growth as problem solvers.

As students become stuck during classroom problem-solving experiences, teachers can guide them with suggestions and encouragement. It is especially important, however, that after the problem has been solved, students are asked to reflect on how they got "unstuck." Asking students what they did that proved successful and highlighting those effective strategies for continuing to move forward in the problem-solving process will benefit all students in the class as they share experiences and begin to develop a repertoire of strategies for those frustrating moments.

Following are some self-help strategies for getting "unstuck." Students might develop their own list of strategies based on their experiences and the experiences of their classmates. Similar ideas can be shared with parents during a parent night at school, as shown on the CD, providing them with ideas on how to guide their children through home problem-solving activities.

Jot Down Ideas

Jot down a plan for how you will be solving the problem. You might list the important information or draw a diagram of the problem to get you started.

Restate the Problem in Your Own Words

Are you unsure how to begin? Reread the problem and then say it in your own words. You need to understand the problem before you can go any further.

Cross Off Unnecessary Information

Is the problem confusing, containing too much data? Reread the problem and cross out the unnecessary data to simplify the problem.

Substitute with Simpler Numbers

Does the problem contain large numbers or fractions or decimals that are confusing you? Substitute simpler numbers for the confusing numbers and then figure out how to solve the problem. Once you know how the problem should be solved, just plug the more complicated numbers back into the problem and repeat the process to solve it.

Take a Break

Are you too frustrated to go on? Take a break for a few minutes. Think about or do something else. Then return to the problem refreshed and ready to begin again.

Use a Manipulative

Use everyday objects (paper clips, toothpicks, pennies) to represent the items in the problem. Act out the problem with the manipulatives.

Talk the Problem Through

Talk out loud to yourself or to someone else. Explain the problem and what you think you should do. Listen to yourself as you talk to see if what you say makes sense.

Think of a Similar Problem

Does this problem remind you of another that you've solved? How did you solve that one? Try that strategy. Does it work here?

Try a Different Strategy

What you're doing doesn't seem to be working. Try something else. Is there a different strategy that you think might work? Try it and see.

Give Yourself a Pep Talk

Think of a problem you solved by sticking with it. Remember a time when you were frustrated but kept on trying until you found the answer. Remind yourself that you can do it!

Involving Students in Instruction

Teaching problem solving is teaching students to think in an organized manner. It is the process of helping students recognize how logical and productive thinking works. To make thinking visible to our students, we use techniques such as think-alouds, co-operative learning activities, visual demonstrations, and hands-on practice. By transforming thinking from an abstract idea to a visible activity, we keep students engaged in the lessons, strengthen their understanding, and help them gain the skills they need to become more organized thinkers.

Again, it is important that we model our thinking by speaking aloud to students as we proceed through demonstration problems together. This think-aloud process helps us clearly show our students what goes on in our heads as we think through problem situations. By sharing examples of logical thinking and by modeling thoughtful questions and reasonable conclusions, we highlight for students what should be happening in their own heads during the problem-solving process.

In addition, it is important that students have opportunities to discuss strategies with one another as they formulate and test ideas about how to proceed with each problem (Whitin and Whitin 2000). Cooperative-learning strategies are valuable tools during problem-solving instruction, as they allow students to hear each other's thoughts and help each child expand his or her repertoire of ideas. Working with partners or groups gives students the opportunity to test their ideas on others or analyze their teammates' ideas and solutions. Group work helps students monitor their thinking, analyze their progress, and discuss alternate methods of solving each problem. Working with others also helps reduce the anxiety that often comes with "standing alone" and allows students to take risks and gain confidence in their own abilities. It allows them to practice their thinking in a safe and comfortable environment.

Visual and hands-on demonstrations are also critical in helping students understand problem-solving strategies. We might use an overhead projector, video visualizer, blackboard, or erasable board to demonstrate strategies. Using hands-on materials to simulate a problem or create a diagram helps our students see ways to re-create what is happening in the problem. As students develop an understanding of the strategy, the visual and hands-on examples will naturally give way to more abstract thinking.

Students need repeated practice with problem-solving strategies, and they need to be given opportunities to decide which strategies apply to which problems. After initial exposure to each strategy, the teacher should give students multiple opportunities to look at a mixed group of problems and determine which strategy makes sense in each situation. Students will often remember certain problems that serve as anchor problems. As students realize, "That's just like the pizza problem!," they will begin to connect the new problem to the familiar "pizza" problem and recognize that applying the same strategy may be successful. During these types of activities, our students need opportunities to hear each other's ideas and discuss the appropriateness of specific strategies, because often more than one strategy may be effective. In the following chapters, we explore the development of problem-solving strategies in greater detail.

And, connecting problem-solving instruction to real-world experiences and data helps students recognize the purpose for learning each strategy. Throughout this book, you will see an emphasis on using real-world problems during problem-solving instruction. During early instruction, problems should reflect the interests of the students and may deal with games, pets, or food. As students become more adept at problem solving, they are better able to deal with the challenge of real data. Unlike textbook word problems, real-world problems are not always clear-cut, easily defined, and composed of simple numbers. Students are faced with making sense of real data as they attempt to solve the problem, which prepares them for future problem-solving experiences in a way that textbooks and worksheets are unable to do.

A Word About Word Problems

When we think of problem solving, most of us think about traditional word problems. Word problems of the past were written in a very prescriptive and predictable way (i.e., There were 120 adults and 240 children at the concert. How many people were at the concert altogether?). These tasks were termed *word problems* to distinguish them from routine computational tasks. Word problems often appeared at the end of the page in our textbooks or at the end of a chapter. The problems were generally predictable. If we had been working on adding fractions for the past two weeks, it was likely that we would add the fractions that appeared in the word problems. We often didn't need to process the information as it was so directly related to the computations we had been practicing. Word problems got a bad name as they were often not problems at all, since the skill was immediately recognizable and the solutions simple to find.

In today's math classrooms, we have expanded and extended our concept of problem solving. Today's word problems strive to push students' thinking with problems that represent more complex situations, require more thinking to find solutions and even may result in multiple answers. They may be short or long, but always push students to think to find a solution. Some are certainly more complex than others; however, even simple problems can be meaningful and present foundational skills that will later serve our students well as they attempt to solve complex problems. The term *word problems* does not have to be limited to the old-fashioned ones we remember in our textbooks. Problems are in words, because words express ideas and present situations. In equations, the numbers and symbols are written out for us, telling us which operation to use and on which numbers we should be using it. That makes it a rote process. In word problems, the words provide us with a situation and we must decide which data is important, what we are being asked to do, and how we will proceed to find a solution. It is the words that make it challenging and that invite us to think beyond rote. And it is words (discussions and writing) that allow us to teach and explore the problem situations. Consider the following word problem that does not look like our word problems of the past:

Julie wants to buy a candy bar that costs $0.25. What combinations of coins could she use?

To find a solution, students must have an understanding of money, an ability to compute with monetary values, a knowledge of which operation might help them, and an ability to organize all of the data to avoid confusion. Our goal is to balance simple tasks with more complex, extended tasks in order to continue to challenge students' thinking. Whether we call them word problems, story problems, or simply problem-solving activities, they are tasks in which the solution is not immediately apparent and tasks that challenge students to think and to apply their math skills. In the following chapters, we explore critical strategies that support students to solve simple as well as increasingly complex problems.

CLASSROOM-TESTED TIP

Estimating the Answer

Once students have decided on their plan for solving a problem, it is a good time for them to stop and think about what the predicted answer will be. When students are able to predict or estimate the answer, they are better able to judge the reasonableness of the answer when they calculate it later in the process. Many errors occur when students make calculation mistakes and have not previously considered what the answer might be. Without a predicted answer, an inappropriate calculation may not be noticed. Seeing a discrepancy between his or her predicted answer and a calculated answer sends up a red flag, alerting the student to take a second look at the answer.

There may be times when predicting an answer is difficult. It is easy to do some quick mental math to estimate that the sum of 52 and 131 will be about 180. But for some problems, for example those for which a diagram might be needed to find a solution, it will be difficult for students to predict. Predicting is a step that can help students later in the process. If they are unable to do it, it's okay; teach students to move on and continue with the remaining steps in the problem-solving process.

CLASSROOM-TESTED TIP

Modeling Your Thinking

The think-aloud is a valuable tool when teaching problem solving. During a think-aloud, the teacher says aloud what she is thinking while working through the problem. The teacher verbalizes more than the math content, she also verbalizes when she is confused and what she does as a result of the confusion, or verbalizes her insights and discoveries as she observes math data. In a think-aloud, students are able to hear the teacher's thoughts as she analyzes the situation and makes decisions:

> *"Let's see—I know that every basket has the same number of apples in it. That tells me I can use multiplication. I'll just look back at the question to check how many apples are in each basket."*
>   or
> *"I predicted that the answer would be 12, but I got 130. Something is not right. It wouldn't make sense for the answer to be 130. I think I'll go back and check my calculations to see if I made a mistake."*

Teachers who are cognizant of common errors can direct their think-alouds to those mistakes.

Questions for Discussion

1. How do the word problems you remember from your days as a student compare to the word problems that your current students face?

2. How can attention to the steps of the problem-solving process support students as they attempt to solve problems?

3. What are some key instructional techniques to help students recognize effective problem-solving thinking?

4. Many students get stuck during their attempts to solve problems. What tips for getting "unstuck" might be helpful to them? How might these ideas be shared?

Focusing on Problem-Solving Strategies

As with any other component of the mathematical tool kit, strategies must receive instructional attention if students are expected to learn them.

—National Council of Teachers of Mathematics,
Principles and Standards for School Mathematics

For some of our students, thinking skills come easily. These students are naturally able to organize ideas, represent concepts, adjust predictions, and draw conclusions. For many others, exposure to, experience with, and reflection about their thinking is vital. It may be difficult for them to determine where to begin on a problem, how to simplify a problem, or how to effectively move through the problem to a solution. While one student might view a problem as easy, another sees the same problem as difficult—unable to determine an approach that will lead him or her to the answer. Many students judge problems as difficult or confusing only because they lack the skills to plan an approach, organize the ideas, and ultimately, simplify the problem. Knowledge of problem-solving strategies provides our students with the tools to simplify problems.

The Importance of Problem-Solving Strategies

Problem-solving strategies are what we do in our heads as we make sense of and solve problems. They are our tools for simplifying problems and revealing the possible paths to solutions. Focusing on the development of problem-solving strategies is about helping students understand and employ sound thinking processes, an important goal of mathematics instruction. It is the understanding of these thinking processes, combined with a knowledge of math skills and an understanding of math concepts, that allows our students to effectively solve problems. As our students are challenged to solve problems about fractions, their understanding of the concept of fractions and their knowledge of how to add, subtract, multiply, or divide fractions is important, but without the thinking skills to analyze the problem situation and determine which fractions to use and which operation to apply, students would be unable to find a solution. The better our students understand their own thinking and continue to develop that thinking, the more confident they are during problem-solving tasks. This focus on understanding their own thinking (metacognition) is a critical goal of good problem-solving instruction.

Much has been written about the teaching of problem-solving strategies. While there are some variations in the names of the strategies, there is much agreement regarding the critical-thinking skills that play a key role in math problem solving, and therefore deserve attention in our math classrooms. The names that have been given to the key problem-solving strategies are simple and are intended to capture the essence of the thinking skills (Choose an Operation, Find a Pattern, Make a Table, Make an Organized List, Draw a Picture or Diagram, Use Logical Reasoning, Guess, Check, and Revise, and Work Backward). Because the names are quite simple, however, it should not be misinterpreted that these skills are simple. While they can be presented in a simple form to younger students, they continue to develop in complexity and support students at all grade levels as they attempt to solve even the most complex of problems.

Beneath the simple strategy names lies an array of important skills that empower students to be more effective problem solvers. Good problem solvers understand the operations and can recognize them in problem situations (Choose an Operation). Good problem solvers observe numbers and recognize relationships between numbers whether patterns or functional relationships (Find a Pattern, Make a Table). Good problem solvers can organize data to work through problems in systematic ways (Make a Table, Make an Organized List, Draw a Picture or Diagram). Good problem solvers can use inverse thinking when necessary to find a solution (Work Backward). Good problem solvers can make sense of a seeming overload of information and can organize it and draw conclusions from it (Draw a Picture or Diagram, Use Logical Reasoning). Good problem solvers take risks, and use their number sense combined with trial-and-error thinking to proceed toward a solution (Guess, Check, and Revise). The simple problem-solving strategies are not simple at all, but represent significant thinking skills. Students who become adept at these thinking skills are armed with the tools they need to face many and varied problems.

As we explore problem-solving strategies throughout this book, it is important to remember that we are not teaching or telling students to use a particular strategy, but rather helping them develop the thinking skills to find an appropriate strategy for solving a problem. Often more than one strategy will lead to a solution. Students' work should be evaluated based on the reasonableness of the strategy, not whether it was the strategy we may have had in mind as we posed the problem. Fourth-grade students worked on the following problem:

Kelly bought 8 cookies at the school bake sale. Cookies were sold in bags of 2 cookies for 75 cents. How much did 8 cookies cost?

The student work samples in Figure 3–1 show different, but both appropriate, strategies for solving the problem. While one student used a picture followed by addition to find the solution, the other simply recognized the problem as a multiplication task. Still others in the class created tables to solve the problem. Sharing the varied ways that students solve problems enlightens others in the class to possible methods. As we help students recognize and employ varied problem-solving approaches we are helping them build a repertoire of problem-solving strategies, which is the utimate goal for each of our students (NCTM 1989).

Keys to Developing Strategies

Within a single classroom, students' abilities to understand and apply strategies may differ dramatically. While some students intuitively apply the strategies, others may be at a beginning level in their understanding. These strategies do not develop by grade

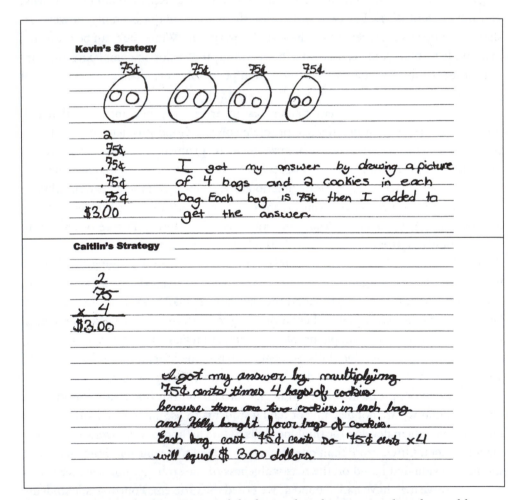

Figure 3–1 *Kevin drew a picture of the bags of cookies to visualize the problem and recognize the need for addition, while Caitlin applied her understanding of multiplication to solve the same problem.*

level, but by experience with and exposure to this type of thinking. A third-grade student who has had many opportunities to explore and discuss the strategies may show greater development than a fifth-grade student who has had limited exposure to this type of thinking. An understanding of the development of these strategies from simple to complex benefits teachers at all grade levels and provides us with critical knowledge to adjust our instruction. With a deep understanding of these strategies, we are able to break down the skills to support our struggling students or layer on sophistication to challenge our more proficient problem solvers.

Attention to the development of problem-solving strategies should be a component of math instruction at all grade levels. As students move through the grades, these thinking skills are refined and enhanced. While third-grade students might explore organized lists through simple problems about combinations between three colors of shoes and three colors of socks, fifth-grade students might explore organized lists through more sophisticated tasks like finding all of the combinations of nickels, dimes, and quarters that equal 50 cents. The essential thinking skills (finding a systematic way to move through the data and record the information) are similar, but the latter is more complicated requiring additional thought and more complex math skills. Facility with problem-solving strategies does not develop in a single lesson, but rather continues to develop over the years as students experience and explore problems of increasing sophistication. It is the understanding of the progression of these skills, from simple to complex, that allows teachers to effectively meet students' needs and help them refine and extend their understanding of each strategy. As you explore the practice problems on the CD you will notice the increasing complexity wthin each set of problems and will be able to differentiate lessons by choosing problems based on the needs of your students.

In grades 3 through 5, it is a good practice to introduce each strategy. While some students may have seen and discussed the strategies before, others may be seeing them for the first time. Beginning at a simple level will help students experience success and will provide an opportunity to discuss the underlying thinking skills. Visual or hands-on activities are particularly useful in helping students visualize the strategy.

Once students have been introduced to each strategy, frequent practice tasks provide opportunities for them to revisit the skills. Quality is better than quantity in practice sessions, as we place more emphasis on talking through a few problems rather than simply completing many problems. Questions like, "What strategy did you use to solve that problem?" "How did you know to use that strategy?" and "What was confusing about that problem and what did you do to make it easier?" should be frequently heard in third- through fifth-grade classrooms. Prompting our students to think about similar problems with prompts like, "When have we seen something like this before?" or "Does this problem remind you of any you have done before?" will help them improve their skills in selecting appropriate strategies.

Stimulating communication about these thinking strategies is a key component of developing the skills. Students' metacognitive skills increase as they are challenged to think about and express their own thinking. Students should be frequently asked to explain, justify, and reflect on their problem solving. Prompts like those in Figure 3–2 will push students' thinking.

Ask students to explain how they solve problems.

- List the steps you used to solve this problem.
- Explain how you solved this problem.
- What might be another way to solve this problem?

Ask students to justify their answers or their decisions.

- Which strategy did you choose? Why do you think that strategy was a good choice for solving this problem?
- Justify why you believe your answer is correct.
- Explain why you set up your (table, diagram, list, etc.) the way you did.

Ask students to write problems of their own.

- Write a problem that can be solved using (multiplication, division, working backward, etc.).
- Write a problem that can be solved by using a table (or finding a pattern or drawing a picture, etc.).
- Write a problem about 24×17.
- Write a problem that requires several steps in order to be solved.

Ask students to reflect on their strengths, weaknesses, and feelings as they learn problem solving.

- What was easy about solving this problem? What was hard?
- What are you still confused about? Do you have any questions that need to be answered?
- Now I understand . . .
- I get frustrated when . . .
- When I don't know what to do I . . .
- I discovered that . . .
- Next time I will . . .

Figure 3–2 *Talking and Writing About Problem Solving*

Through teacher talk and think-alouds, student-to-student discussions about problems, whole-class debriefings after problem solving, and opportunities to write about their insights and experiences, students begin to hear each other's ideas and practice expressing their own. It is during these communication activities that the simple strategy names (e.g., Find a Pattern, Use Logical Reasoning, Work Backward) serve to support our students because they now have words to express the abstract thinking processes they are experiencing. Describing thinking is not always easy for our students. One fourth grader, when asked to explain how he got his answer, exclaimed, "I guessed and checked!" "What do you mean?" the teacher asked. "I didn't know what it was but I guessed 16 and 17 cause I thought it was about that, but I added and those were too high so I tried lower numbers and found the answer." This simple strategy name allowed him to find words to describe his thinking processes.

Exploring the Strategies in Detail

While most textbooks and curricula contain problems focused on these strategies, assigning these problem tasks will not teach these skills. It is the selection of problems combined with discussion, exploration, and reflection that supports students as they develop an understanding of problem-solving strategies. While we were all assigned problems, we were not all taught how to solve math problems. It is the way in which we explore and illustrate the strategies that is most important to the development of our students' skills. In the following chapters, we explore each strategy in more detail. We look at visual, hands-on, and interactive ways to present, explore, and discuss a variety of problem-solving strategies so that students will be able to understand and apply the strategies to make sense of and solve a wide range of math problems.

CLASSROOM-TESTED TIP

Problem-Solving Journals

A problem of the week might be posed for students to record and solve in a math journal. Students' solutions, as well as their reflections about those solutions (how they solved it, which strategy they used), are recorded. Students can then be asked to share their work with a partner (see Figure 3–3) or might present a problem and solution to the class during a group sharing.

Teachers might have students record a demonstration problem for each strategy in their journal—one that was discussed with the whole class. The journals will then be a place for "familiar" problems—those benchmark problems that students explored together—and serve to remind them of a problem that illustrates each strategy.

Problem-solving journals are a great way to document students' progress in the development of problem-solving skills. They make handy artifacts for parent conferences or workshops and allow parents to view the types of problems their children are exploring, as well as provide a glimpse into their own child's strengths and weaknesses. And they are a wonderful way for students to see their own progress over the course of the school year.

(*Note:* A journal does not have to be a bound book—it may be a collection of papers that teachers bind for students or pages that are placed in a section of a binder.)

Figure 3–3 *Journals allow students to record their ideas and share them with others.*

C L A S S R O O M - T E S T E D   T I P

Problem-Solving Icons

As students attempt to select an appropriate strategy for solving a problem, the use of icons (pictures to represent the strategies) can serve to remind them of the strategies they have explored in class (see Figure 3–4). A bulletin board or special area of the classroom can be designated to display icons. As students explore a specific strategy, an icon for that strategy is posted. Additional icons are posted as students build their repertoire of strategies. Throughout the year, as students attempt to solve problems, the teacher can direct their attention to the icons as reminders of possible solution strategies. See Strategy Icons on the CD for reproducible icons to post in your classroom or Strategy Bookmarks on the CD for a template to create math bookmarks that display the icons for student reference during class or homework assignments.

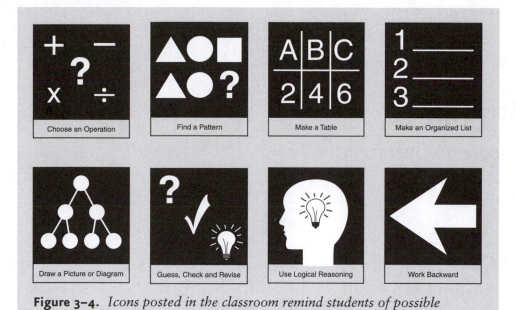

Figure 3–4. *Icons posted in the classroom remind students of possible strategies for solving math problems.*

Questions for Discussion

1. In what ways can students benefit from understanding their own thinking (metacognition) and recognizing which problem-solving strategies they are using?

2. Why is it important to help students build a repertoire of strategies?

3. What is the role of communication (talk and writing) in developing problem-solving strategies?

4. Why might it be important for a teacher to understand the progression of skills in these problem-solving strategies?

4

Strategy

Choose an Operation

Understanding the fundamental operations of addition, subtraction, multiplication, and division is central to knowing mathematics. One essential component of what it means to understand an operation is recognizing conditions in real-world situations that indicate that the operation would be useful in those situations.

—National Council of Teachers of Mathematics,
Curriculum and Evaluation Standards for School Mathematics

We acknowledge the importance of helping students understand the problem-solving process, the way to proceed through a problem from start to finish. We recognize that students must be able to identify the question or determine what they are being asked to find out before they can effectively find a solution. But we also recognize that once students know what they are being asked to solve, they must be able to consider varied approaches and decide on a plan that makes sense for that problem. Choosing an operation is one of the strategies that students might employ in order to find a solution. Addition, subtraction, multiplication, and division are methods of finding the solution to many math problems. Determining which of these operations is appropriate for solving a problem is a critical, and frequently used, problem-solving strategy.

Students' ability to select the correct operation when solving word problems can often be a reflection of the way in which they were taught each operation. Students who memorized math facts without developing a clear understanding of the concepts may have more difficulty identifying when each operation should be used than those students who developed an understanding of each concept through demonstrations, explanations, and hands-on experiences. In the initial teaching of each operation, it is imperative that students understand the concept of when to use that operation.

When students begin to learn about multiplication, for example, it is important that they see and hear situations in which groups of equal size are put together to form a larger group. After repeatedly experiencing the concept, students are able to understand the operation involved in 3×4, rather than just knowing that the answer is 12 because of repeated flash card practice.

Key Words Versus Key Concepts

Even though teachers often use key words as a method of assisting students in choosing an appropriate operation, be careful about teaching students to rely solely on key words (Sowder 2002). It is often true that when the word *altogether* appears in a problem, it is an addition problem. Those words, however, can appear in other problems, and students who look for one or two familiar words but do not stop to analyze the entire problem may incorrectly determine that addition is the operation to use. Consider the problem:

> **The third- and fourth-grade classes were on the playground for recess. There were 65 students on the playground altogether. 17 of them went back to their classrooms to work on a special project. How many students were on the playground?**

While the word *altogether* does appear, it is not an indication of the correct operation as this is clearly a subtraction problem. Asking students to think about what is happening in the problem (some students are leaving a group) will help them determine that subtraction is the appropriate operation. Particularly with the increase in real-world problem-solving tasks and more complex performance tasks, there may be several key words within a problem that will mislead the student who is relying only on key words.

Students should look for key concepts rather than key words. After reading the problem, they should visualize the situation rather than focusing on a word or phrase in hopes that it will tell them how to proceed. Understanding the key concepts for each operation will help students make a thoughtful decision regarding the appropriate operation to use in solving the problem.

Practice with Recognizing Key Concepts

Addition

Addition is the process of putting things together. The sets do not need to be equal. Rather than focusing on the key word *altogether*, keep in mind that it is the concept of *altogether* (bringing groups together or joining parts to make a whole), not the word, that tells a student that it is time to add. If you are trying to find out the total number of people who will be attending a concert, you add the number of children and the number of adults to find the total number of people in attendance.

Addition is an appropriate operation to use to find out the total number of items even if each group is equal. If we are trying to decide the total number of students in the gym, and there are six teams with seven students on each team, we can find it by adding 7 + 7 + 7 + 7 + 7 + 7, although multiplication is a faster way to find the answer for those students who have developed an understanding of that operation. Primary teachers help students understand addition as they place groups of objects on the overhead and physically pull them together or use physical demonstrations in the classroom with groups of students to illustrate the concept. And certainly primary students should have experiences using desktop manipulatives to illustrate basic addition problems. By third through fifth grade, students should have a general understanding of addition however, as numbers become more complex (e.g., fractions, decimals, large numbers), students greatly benefit from hands-on experiences and visual demonstrations to extend their understanding of the operation of addition (as well as the other operations). Using fraction pieces to demonstrate addition of fractions or allowing students to explore with base-ten blocks as they develop an understanding of adding decimals will help them better understand the concept of addition.

Subtraction

Subtraction can be more difficult for students to understand because there are several models for subtraction. The most commonly taught is the *take-away* model. Whenever something is removed from a group, we subtract. Students pick this concept up quickly. If there were 50 pieces of candy in a bag and we ate 13 of them, subtraction would help us find out how many pieces of candy were left in the bag. Another very important model for subtraction is the *compare* model. Whenever items are compared, we use subtraction to find the difference between them. If we are asking students to determine how much one object is taller, wider, or heavier than another, they would subtract to find the difference. Reminding students that whenever they compare, they should subtract will help them master this concept. Another phrase often used in subtraction problems asks a child to determine "how many more" of something are needed to make two quantities equal. This is a form of comparison. For example, a comparison problem could read:

> **If Katie had 26 baseball cards and Michael had 17 baseball cards, how many more cards would Michael need to buy to have the same amount as Katie?**

Using overhead counters and lining up the two rows next to each other to allow students to see the difference between the two groups helps them visualize this comparison model.

Multiplication

The concept of multiplication can be easily demonstrated with real objects, manipulatives, or overhead materials. Like addition, multiplication is used to find the total number of objects; however, when using multiplication, all sets must have the same number of objects. If there are 6 cartons of eggs and each carton has 12 eggs in it, multiplication can be used to find the total number of eggs. Using manipulatives to construct equal groups and then pulling the groups together on an overhead or on students' desktops will visually demonstrate the concept of multiplication. And the frequent use of story problems helps students continue to experience multiplication scenarios.

Division

Division is an operation about which students often become confused. Again, a visual representation will help students see that in division we are starting with a whole group and then splitting that group into smaller, equal groups. No objects are removed from the group, as in the take-away model of subtraction. Division asks how many smaller groups are formed or how many items are in each smaller group. While the groups that are formed have equal quantities, it is important that students understand that remainders may result.

Posters or signs in the classroom can help remind students of the key concepts for each operation as shown in the Key Concepts Posters on the CD. It is important to remind students that it is not the key words that indicate which operation to use, but the key concepts or ideas. We are not looking for the word *altogether*, because it will not appear in all addition or multiplication problems. We are looking for the concept of putting things together. When students are able to identify the concept, they will be able to successfully choose the appropriate operation.

Practice with Choosing the Correct Operation

Group Activities and Discussions

It is important for students to have opportunities to practice selecting the appropriate operation. This can be done through pair and group activities in which students are given a team problem and asked to determine the correct operation. As students discuss which operation they would choose and why, they are able to hear each other's ideas and strengthen their understanding of the key concepts. When sharing their answers with the rest of the class, students should always include a justification for their choice of operations, telling why they chose the operation they did.

Pinch Cards

Pinch cards, a form of all-pupil response, also provide practice in identifying the correct operation. All students receive their own card. Beginning third graders might work with a card that has only addition and subtraction operation signs, adding multiplication and division as they begin to discuss those concepts. Fourth- and fifth-grade students would work with a card that includes all four operation signs. Teachers can

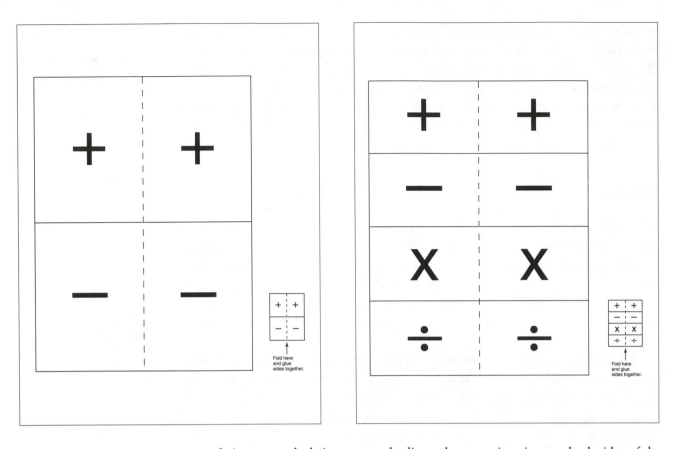

 create their own cards, being sure to duplicate the operation signs on both sides of the cards, or use the Pinch Cards samples on the CD. The operation signs should be placed in the same location on the front and back of the card, so students can see the sign from the back of the card while teachers see the same sign from the front. As the teacher poses a problem, students pinch (hold the card by that sign) the operation they would use to solve the problem. The teacher then briefly asks students to justify their decisions. This allows a quick, interactive review that students enjoy, and it allows teachers to quickly spot those students who are still having difficulty with the concepts. Those students may be pulled aside later for review or reteaching.

Student-Created Problems

Asking students to develop their own problems related to sets of data is another way to help them strengthen their skills at understanding the operations. Give students a set of data and ask them to create a real problem that might use the data. For example, students may write a variety of problems using the following data.

Data: 8 slices of pizza, $1.50 per slice of pizza, 4 children

Sample student-created problems include:

"There were 8 slices of pizza and 4 children. If they shared equally, how many pieces would each child get?"

"The children bought 8 slices of pizza. Each slice costs $1.50. How much did they spend?"

"Three children had one slice of pizza each. The other child ate the rest. How many slices did he eat?"

"One child bought a slice of pizza and paid with a $5.00 bill. How much change did he get back?"

"Kathy had a $5.00 bill. How many slices of pizza could she buy?"

After students write their story problems, have them present the problems to their group or to the entire class. Students might trade problems between partners or groups and solve each other's problems. Students can be asked to sort the problems by operation. Some of the student-written problems might be used for class problem-solving warm-ups over the next few days. Asking students to explain how they knew which operation they should use to solve each problem is a critical part of the thinking process.

Focusing on Increasingly Complex Problems

The complexity of math problems increases in grades 3 through 5 and helping students understand and solve more complex problems becomes an important component of problem-solving instruction. Rather than the simple one-step problems that were posed in the primary grades, intermediate students are faced with problems that may be multistep, require students to select appropriate data from a set of data, or even convert data in order to find solutions. Exploring ways in which problems become more complex, and helping our students recognize and solve these problems, is an important role of the intermediate problem-solving teacher.

During the intermediate grades, students are often faced with finding the data they need to solve a problem. Sometimes unnecessary data is presented in the problem and students must determine what is needed and what is not needed to find a solution. The following problem contains unnecessary information:

> **The parents in Mrs. King's class donated cookies and brownies to sell at the school carnival. 200 people came to the carnival. Cookies were sold for $0.25 each and brownies were sold for $0.50 each. They sold 120 cookies and 140 brownies. How much money did they collect?**

Students do not need to know that 200 people came to the carnival, and yet that data appears in the problem and often confuses students who are unsure of which data to use. The ability to identify unnecessary information is a critical problem-solving skill. Students need to be able to understand the question being asked and to identify the data that specifically addresses that question. Focusing on identifying unnecessary information is essentially focusing on whether students *know the question* and *know the data needed to find an answer*. Asking students to state what they are trying to find out and what they already know helps to focus them on the connection between the data and the question. Teachers might ask students to cross out unnecessary data in the problem. Asking them to clarify why the data is not needed helps ensure their understanding. Calley said that she did not need to know that 200 people came to the carnival. When asked to explain why that was unnecessary she confidently stated, "because I only needed to know how many people bought cookies and brownies to find out how much money they made, not how many people were there." Calley understood what she was being asked to solve and was able to identify the data that would get her to a solution.

Problems in grades 3 through 5 often provide students with a bank of data from which to choose. Consider the problem that asks students to determine which is cheaper, milk and a cookie or lemonade and a cupcake? Students need to use the menu data to locate the appropriate data and then use it to solve the problem.

Sam's Snack Shop Menu

Cookies $0.35
Candy Bar $0.75
Popcorn $0.80
Cupcakes $0.65
Soda $0.90
Lemonade $1.25
Milk $1.35

Students must now select the needed data from a set of data and then know how to proceed to solve the problem. Understanding that they must combine (add) the price of milk and a cookie and then combine (add) the price of lemonade and a cupcake, and then compare those costs to each other (subtract), requires the selection of appropriate data, the understanding of operations, and the ability to do multistep tasks.

In multistep problems, students are required to interpret and solve a problem that has multiple components. Students might be asked to solve the following problem:

> **Jenny bought two slices of pizza that cost $1.50 each, one soda that costs $1.25, and 3 cookies that cost $0.45 each. Her mother gave her a $10.00 bill. Will she have enough money to pay for her food? Justify your answer with math data.**

Students are required to apply a variety of skills in order to successfully solve multistep problems. Rather than the simple primary problems in which they may have recognized the operation of addition and added the only two numbers within the problem, they now need a deeper understanding of these more complex problems including the ability to identify significant data, know what to do with that data, and understand and proceed through a series of steps that lead to a solution. In the previous problem, students might multipy the cost by the quantity to find the cost of the two slices of pizza or the three cookies, but will still need to add the cost of the pizza, cookies, and soda to find the total spent on the food. But even then, they are not done, because they need to compare the cost of the food with Jenny's $10.00 in order to find out if she will have enough money. And they must be able to justify their decision with math data. Multistep problems require students to apply a variety of math skills as they solve the problem. In helping students understand and effectively solve multistep tasks, teachers might first split the task into parts so that students can find the first solution and then move on the next step. This helps some students gain confidence as well as develop their understanding of the multistep process. Teachers also might ask students to circle or underline the questions being asked in a problem, reminding them that there may be more than one question being asked. And providing opportunities for students to discuss and write about the steps they took to solve more complex problems is critical.

Intermediate problems are also often complicated with conversions, forcing students to apply their understandings of math ideas as well as their computational skills. Some conversion problems might include:

Jack had a square garden. Each side measured 9 feet. What was the perimeter in yards?

Danny bought doughnuts for his class party. There were 32 students and 1 teacher in his class. How many dozen doughnuts did he need to buy so that everyone could have at least 1 doughnut?

In each case, students need to understand the question and how the question data differs from the data being asked for in the solution (i.e., feet vs. yards, individual doughnuts vs. dozen). They also need the computation skills to convert their answers into yards or dozen. The understanding of the measurements and the ability to determine how to make the conversions add to the complexity of the tasks, but isn't that what we hope our students will be able to do: to use their math skills to think through increasingly complex situations? We have lofty goals in problem solving and can become frustrated when our students' thinking doesn't progress quickly, but remembering the complexity and importance of teaching problem solving helps us stay focused on modeling good thinking and supporting our students as they struggle with developing their thinking skills. Continually asking "What do we need to find out?" "What do we know?" "How will the data help us?" "What steps will we need to take to find the solution?" and "Does our answer match the question?" will continue to focus students on key questions to drive their problem-solving experiences.

Frequent talk about methods for approaching multistep tasks will help bolster student understanding. Highlighting the steps needed to find the solution will focus attention on the multistep aspect. We might ask students what should be done first to get us started, or what else we need to figure out in order to continue working toward a solution. Having students work with partners to explore multistep tasks will encourage communication, pushing students to talk about their thinking and share their strategies for moving through the multiple tasks. And frequent and specific feedback on their efforts will provide students with insight into where they might be going off-track or ways in which their hard work and reflection have increased their problem-solving abilities.

A Look at Student Work

The following samples of student writing help to illustrate students' reasoning regarding choosing an appropriate operation. In each case, students have analyzed the problem situation and chosen the operation based on their understanding of the problem, not their recognition of key words that appear in the problem.

Jenny, Jill, and Jane shared a pizza. Jenny ate $\frac{1}{4}$ of the pizza, Jill ate $\frac{1}{8}$ of the pizza, and Jane ate $\frac{1}{8}$ of the pizza. What fraction of the pizza did they eat?

"I added so I could see how much of the pizza all three of them ate. It's like putting the fractions together to see how much it is together." (Even with the complication of fractions, this student recognized the concept of addition.)

In the long jump event, Steven's jump measured 173 centimeters. Melissa jumped 164 centimeters. How many more centimeters would Melissa have had to jump to tie Steven?

"I used subtraction because you need to subtract in order to find the difference between 173 and 164. That's the same number of centimeters more that Melissa would have had to jump in order for there to be a tie." (Notice the idea of comparison!)

Mrs. Singer's students were working in teams for math class. There were 4 students in each team. Mrs. Singer had 7 teams of students in her classroom. How many students were in Mrs. Singer's class?

"I multiplied to find out how many because every team had the same number and when that happens you can multiply and it's faster than adding."

There were 132 students participating in Field Day. The students were split into 12 equal teams. How many students were on each team?

"I chose to divide because when you divide you split things into even groups and that's what I needed to do to solve this problem."

In Figure 4–1, the student was required to understand and apply several operations in order to solve this multistep problem. Her representations and writing show her understanding of the operations of division and addition, as she uses both operations to find the correct solution.

Communicating About the Strategy

Asking students to talk and write about how and why they arrived at an answer or selected an operation helps teachers better assess their understanding of the operations. Allowing students to work in pairs or groups to discuss their choice of operations will help them begin to develop ways to verbalize their thoughts. By listening to others and sharing ideas, they begin to acquire the vocabulary they need to explain their mathematical thinking. It is important to encourage students to put their thoughts in writing to help them process their understanding and help us better assess their knowledge. The student in Figure 4–1 shows her work and explains the multistep process she used to find the answer. Even those students who may require the use of pictures or diagrams to support their explanations will benefit from attempts to "explain their thinking."

Fruit Salad

You decide to make a fruit salad. You want to buy the four fruits
listed below and will need ½ pound of each fruit.

<u>Cost of Fruit</u>
Bananas – 2 pounds for $1.40
Apples - $1.30 per pound
Strawberries - $2.80 per pound
Blueberries - $1.90 per pound

How much will the fruit salad cost? $3.35

Show your work.

4)1.40 Bananas ½ pound cost .35¢ $1.40
                                            .95¢
2)1.30 Apples ½ pound cost .65¢   .65¢
                                         + .35¢
2)2.80 Strawberries ½ pound cost $1.40 $3.35

2)1.90 Blueberries ½ pound cost .95¢

List the steps you took to solve the problem.

First I divided the Bananas cost $1.40 by 4 because
it was 2 pounds for $1.40. Then for the rest
I divided by 2 because it was per pound. After
I got the answers for a half pound for each
I added them and got $3.35 for the fruit
salad.

Figure 4–1 *This student explains the steps she took to solve this multistep task.*

Following are some discussion or writing prompts to extend students' thinking
about operations:

- What operation did you use to solve this problem? Why?

- Explain the steps you used to solve this problem.

- Justify your answer.

- How did you decide on the equation (number sentence) you used to solve this
  problem? Was there another equation that would have also worked?

Selecting Practice Problems

Practice problems using addition, subtraction, multiplication, and division are available in any math book. Students need practice with identifying operations and building appropriate equations to represent problem situations. And continuing to increase
the complexity of the problem tasks through the introduction of multistep problems

or problems with unnecessary information will help develop and refine their problem-solving skills. While these problems can be found in textbooks, keep in mind that real-world problems that connect math to events and situations in students' lives will motivate and excite them. Simple activities like rewording textbook problems to include your students' names or the names of local restaurants, parks, or schools will help to personalize the problem-solving experience. The practice problems provided on the accompanying CD can be modified on your computer prior to printing them. Add your students' names or the names of local businesses and attractions. In addition, using data from local menus, travel brochures, or baseball cards will keep students involved in your lessons and demonstrate the meaningfulness of the mathematics skills they are learning. Real-world problem solving is explored more fully in Chapter 12. Seize any opportunity to make a real-world connection for your students.

CLASSROOM-TESTED TIP

Simplifying Problems

In grades 3 through 5, problems become more complicated for students because the math data is more sophisticated. As fractions, money, decimals, or large numbers appear in problems, students become anxious and confused about how to solve the problem. Show students how to substitute simpler numbers into the problem and then discuss how they might solve the simpler problem. Often students are able to better assess the problem when they are not overwhelmed by the data. Consider the problem:

> The fifth grade was collecting soda cans for a recycling program at school. Mrs. Price's class collected 3,465 cans, Mrs. Beamon's class collected 4,297 cans, and Mrs. Coats' class collected 5,732 cans. How many cans did they collect?

Students might replace the large numbers with simple numbers and then determine their plan for solving the problem.

> The fifth grade was collecting soda cans for a recycling program at school. Mrs. Price's class collected 30 cans, Mrs. Beamon's class collected 40 cans, and Mrs. Coats' class collected 50 cans. How many cans did they collect?

The simpler data allows students to see the problem more clearly. Once they have recognized that addition is a plan for finding the solution, they can go back to the original problem and replace and then add the larger numbers. Teaching students strategies for simplifying problems is an important goal of problem-solving instruction.

CLASSROOM-TESTED TIP

Writing Story Problems

Using equations to prompt students to write story problems is an effective way to assess students' understanding of the basic operations. Provide students with an equation and ask them to create a story problem to match the equation. Consider the following equation: $\$2.50 \times 5 = \$12.50$

> Story: **A ticket to the basketball game costs $2.50. My mother, father, two brothers, and I went to the game. How much did it cost us?**

There are lots of other stories that might go with the same equation.

> Another story: **Jason got an allowance of $2.50 each week. How much money did he have after 5 weeks?**

Writing story problems from equations can be challenging. Allowing students to work with a partner or group provides support for students who are having difficulty creating stories on their own. Students can record their stories in math journals or share their group stories aloud with the whole class. With a thumbs-up response, students can evaluate the stories to see if they match the equation. If stories don't match the equation, classmates can suggest ways to rewrite the story to make it fit. Writing story problems helps students strengthen their understanding of operations.

A variation of this activity is to pair up students and give each student a different equation on an index card. Ask students to turn over the index card so their partners cannot see it. Ask each student to write a story for their equation. When students have finished, have them switch stories with their partners. After reading their partner's story, students must figure out the equation.

Questions for Discussion

1. Why is it important for students to understand the operations?

2. What is the difference between key words and key concepts?

3. How can visual and hands-on activities support students' understanding of operations?

4. What are the difficulties associated with multistep problems? How might teachers support students as problems become more complex?

5

Strategy

Find a Pattern

By continuing to provide a broad variety of opportunities to explore and use patterns, we help students move from a basic recognition of patterns to a more sophisticated use of patterns as a problem-solving strategy.

—Terrence G. Coburn

Patterns are central to our number system. Students begin to recognize and repeat patterns early in their mathematics education. This ability to understand, identify, and extend patterns helps students solve many math problems.

Patterns range from simple to very complex. Students in the primary grades become adept at recognizing patterns with shapes, colors, and simple numbers. They begin to internalize the concept that patterns repeat in a predictable way, and learn to continue the patterns. Primary students explore varied patterns from ab patterns (red–blue, red–blue, red–blue) to aab patterns (red–red–blue, red–red–blue, red–red–blue) to growing patterns (1–2, 1–2–2, 1–2–2–2 . . .), and as students experiment with patterns, they learn to identify the repeating elements and extend the patterns. Students who have experienced a variety of patterns in the primary grades will be better prepared for recognizing and extending the more sophisticated patterns that appear in the intermediate grades.

As students progress to grades 3 through 5, the patterns become increasingly sophisticated and require them to carefully observe and draw conclusions about their observations. These students should be provided with opportunities to explore a variety of patterns in our number system as well as patterns in geometry and other areas of mathematics. Intermediate-level students should be guided to appreciate the power of patterns in solving problems, as it is often through the discovery of a pattern that students are able to progress toward a solution to a problem.

Completing and Describing Number Patterns

Patterns are everywhere in our number system. Beginning with simple patterns and challenging students with increasingly complex number patterns will help them develop a greater understanding of numbers and operations. While many math activities ask students to simply complete a pattern, asking our students to describe patterns extends their thinking and helps us better analyze their understandings. Students describe their understanding of a variety of number patterns below:

2, 4, 8, 16 . . .
"You doubled the number each time."

1, 3, 6, 10 . . .
"First you added one, then two, then three, then four."

2, 1, 3, 2, 4, 3 . . .
"I subtracted one, then added two, then subtracted one, then added two."

1, 2, 3, 5, 8 . . .
"I added the first two numbers to get the next one. I kept adding the last two numbers to get the next one."

When asking students to describe patterns, ask for multiple responses. Patterns can accurately be described in a variety of ways and allowing students to hear different ways allows them to bridge ideas about various operations and better understand the patterns. When describing the pattern 7, 14, 21, 28 . . . , students might say:

> *"I skip-counted by sevens."*
> *"I said all of the multiples of 7."*
> *"I added 7 to each number."*

Each student has accurately described the pattern, but together, the descriptions show connections between operations and illustrate important understandings about numbers. And asking students to take a closer look at patterns and to describe the patterns that they see can lead them to interesting, and often unexpected, insights. When asked to describe the pattern 4, 8, 12, 16, 20, 24, 28, 32 . . . , students responded:

> *"It's like counting by fours."*
> *"It's the answers when you multiply 4×1, 4×2, 4×3, 4×4 . . . "*
> *"It's like adding 4 to the one before it."*
> *"Hey, first they end with a 4, then 8, then 2, then 6, then 0, then it does it again!" (An interesting insight!)*

The more we ask students to look for patterns within our number system, the more patterns they discover!

Making Patterns Visual

While some students have an inate ability to recognize even abstract patterns, other students are greatly supported when they are helped to visualize patterns. Using visual tools like number lines or hundred charts help students see and recognize patterns. Even listing and circling numbers is a simple way to help students visualize a pattern. While students might have difficulty recognizing the pattern 1, 3, 6, 10 . . . , seeing it on a number line can bring about an immediate recognition for students who learn best with visual support.

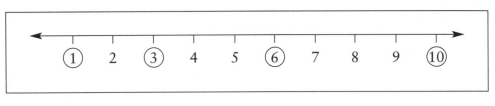

Figure 5–1

This visual allows students to see that first one number is skipped, then two numbers, then three numbers. Moving patterns from abstract to visual is a significant tool for many of our students.

Working with Geometric Patterns

Patterns also exist in the geometric world. As students study shapes and chart sides and angles, they begin to recognize patterns. Take for example the following diagonal problem:

Can you predict how many diagonals can be made in an eight-sided figure?

Students can solve the problem by creating the figure and drawing the diagonals, but they can also solve the problem with an understanding of patterns. After students have drawn a few shapes and counted the diagonals, they will be able to predict the number of diagonals for the remaining shapes based on the pattern they have discovered.

Sides	4	5	6	7	8
Diagonals	2	5	9	14	

Figure 5–2

"I see a pattern. First you added three, then you added four, then you added five. I think you add one more each time. So I would add six this time. My answer is 20 diagonals."

As drawing the figures becomes more difficult, say in the case of an eighteen-sided figure, the use of patterns becomes the preferred—and simpler—way to solve the problem.

Patterns as a Problem-Solving Strategy

Once students become sensitive to searching for patterns, they are able to recognize them in problem situations. And once a pattern is recognized, students have a plan for how to get to the solution—simply continue the pattern to find the solution. This problem shows a simple pattern embedded in a problem task:

> **Kyle and Laura were playing a new video game. Kyle noticed that in the first level of the game, the first score earned two points, the second score earned four points, the third score earned six points, and so on. How much did the eighth score earn?**

Once the pattern is recognized (2, 4, 6 . . .), students can continue it to the eighth place to find the solution. But as always, our goal is to continue to challenge students with increasing complexity. This second part to the problem requires the understanding of a pattern that is less apparent:

> **Laura reached the second level of the game and noticed that at this level, the first score earned two points, the second score earned four points, the third score earned eight points, and the fourth score earned sixteen points. How much did the eighth score earn?**

Students now have to recognize the doubling (or multiplying by two) pattern and again extend it to the eighth place to find the solution. And pattern problems continue to get more complex when patterns merely provide data with which students must solve the problem like in the following:

> **The museum gathered information about the average number of visitors who enter each day. The museum hours are 10:00 A.M. to 6:00 P.M. During the first hour each day an average of 20 people enter the museum. An average of 35 people enter during the second hour, and an average of 50 people enter during the third hour. During the fourth hour, an average of 65 people enter. The museum staff noticed that this pattern continued throughout the day. What is the average number of people who visit the museum each day?**

Now the recognition and extension of the pattern merely provide the data needed for solving the problem. Students must still use their understanding of operations, their computational skills, and their knowledge of elapsed time to complete the task. Patterns become one piece, although a critical piece, to solving the problem.

A Look at Student Work

As students read and analyze problems, they often recognize a pattern within the data. Recognizing and being able to extend the pattern leads them to a solution. Being able to visualize the pattern, so that the data can be analyzed and better understood, can be a challenge for some students. Figures 5–3 and 5–4 are examples of the different ways

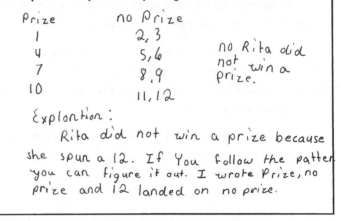

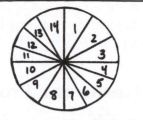

Spin the Wheel

At the school carnival, there was a prize wheel. Each student got to spin the wheel one time to see if they won a prize. Spinning a "one" won a prize. Spinning a "two" or "three" did not win anything. Spinning a "four" won a prize. Spinning a "five" or "six" did not win anything. Spinning a "seven" won a prize. Rita spun a 12. Did she win a prize? Explain how you figured out the answer.

Prize   no Prize

1   2, 3

4   5, 6   no Rita did

7   8, 9   not win a prize.

10   11, 12

Explantion:

     Rita did not win a prize because she spun a 12. If You follow the patter you can figure it out. I wrote Prize, no prize and 12 landed on no prize.

Figure 5–3 *This student sorts data into columns in order to analyze it.*

in which two fourth-grade students recorded their data in order to visualize the pattern. Both students were presented with the same problem, but each chose to record his or her data in a different, yet equally organized, way. And each student was then able to explain how the pattern helped him or her arrive at the answer.

Simply extending a pattern does not always reveal the answer to a problem. In the problem shown in Figure 5–5, the student had to recognize the pattern and extend it and then had to add the data to determine the total race time. Her understanding of patterns helped her compile the needed data so she could move to the next step to find the solution.

Communicating About the Strategy

Asking students to write or talk about creating or extending patterns is a great way to extend their thinking and assess their understanding of patterns. Try prompts like these:

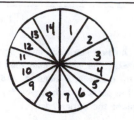

Spin the Wheel

    At the school carnival, there was a prize wheel. Each
student got to spin the wheel one time to see if they won
a prize. Spinning a "one" won a prize. Spinning a "two" or
"three" did not win anything. Spinning a "four" won a
prize. Spinning a "five" or "six" did not win anything.
Spinning a "seven" won a prize. Rita spun a 12. Did she
win a prize? Explain how you figured out the answer.

Example
————

①23④ 567⑧9⑩ 11 12

No she did not. I found my anser
by knowing the first number(1)wins
and the next two don't. And then
the number after the two wins
and the next two numbers dont
and so on. I followed this pattern
all the way to 12 and found out
that 12 dosint win!

Figure 5–4 *This student circles significant data to look
for a pattern.*

■ Describe the pattern.

■ Explain how understanding patterns helped you solve this problem.

■ Is solving problems using patterns easy or hard? Explain your answer.

■ How did an understanding of patterns help you find the data you needed to solve
the problem?

■ If a new student entered the room who did not know anything about patterns,
how would you explain what they are and how they can help you solve problems? Give an example to help them understand.

The Race

Andrew ran a six mile race. He ran the first mile in seven minutes. The second mile took him 7 1/2 minutes to run. He ran the third mile in 8 minutes, and the fourth mile in 8 1/2 minutes. Use the pattern to help you figure out how long it took him to complete the entire race.

$$7 + 7\tfrac{1}{2} + 8 + 8\tfrac{1}{2} + 9 + 9\tfrac{1}{2}$$

Andrew ran the entire race in 49 minutes, 30 *seconds*.

Describe the pattern in the problem. *The pattern shows every mile, the minutes go up (30 seconds.)*

How did knowing the pattern help you figure out the answer? *Knowing the pattern helped me figure out the answer because every time a mile passed, it took an extra 30 seconds, and you had to add on the seconds and minutes. I found it out by adding 7:00 + 7:30 + 8:00 + 8:30 + 9:00 + 9:30 which equals 49 minutes 30 seconds.*

Figure 5–5 *In this problem, recognizing the pattern provided the student with the data needed to solve the problem.*

C L A S S R O O M - T E S T E D   T I P

Hundred Chart Patterns

Divide students into eight groups and have each group color in a hundred chart for multiples of 2, 3, 4, 5, 6, 7, 8, and 9. Each group colors in its hundred chart for a different set of multiples (e.g., one group colors all of the multiples of 6). Have them first use a pencil to place a checkmark in each box that will be colored to avoid coloring errors. After they have finished coloring their chart, have them talk to their group members about observations and insights as they look at the completed chart. Have them share their pattern with the class (see Figure 5–6). Ask the class to compare the charts: How are they alike? How are they different?

Ask students to color in another hundred chart for independent work. They may pick the criteria for their chart. Some ideas include:

- two-digit numbers with a 7 as the ones digit

- two-digit numbers that add up to 6 (e.g., 15, 24 . . .)

- odd numbers

- two-digit numbers in which the ones digit is two more than the tens digit (e.g., 13, 24, 35, 46, . . .)

- two-digit numbers that have two of the same digit (e.g., 22, 33, 44 . . .)

- numbers that have at least one digit that is a 3

Encourage students to be creative. Have them describe their patterns on the bottom or back of their hundred charts. Display the completed hundred chart patterns. (Hundred chart activities adapted from *About Teaching Mathematics* by Marilyn Burns.)

Figure 5–6 *These students share the patterns created by coloring the multiples of a given number.*

CLASSROOM-TESTED TIP

Pattern Cover Up

Explore patterns through an interactive classroom activity in which students try to determine the missing numbers in a pattern. Write a number pattern on the blackboard, chart paper, or overhead projector. Use sticky notes to cover each of the numbers in the sequence (a pattern with five numbers works well). The goal is for students to try to predict the number that is under the last sticky note. Start by removing one sticky note (any one except for the last one), and have students record the number sequence that they predict is hidden under the sticky notes. Ask students to share what they believe is the final number in the sequence, having them justify their prediction by stating the five numbers and describing the pattern.

e.g., ___, ___, 30, ___, ___

One student might predict 50 as the final number stating that the pattern is counting by tens: 10, 20, 30, 40, *50*. Another student might predict 40 as the final number in the pattern and describe the pattern as multiples of 5 starting at 20: 20, 25, 30, 35, *40*. Still another student might predict that 10 is the final number as he describes the pattern as subtracting 10 each time beginning with 50: 50, 40, 30, 20, *10*.

After several students have had a chance to share and discuss their predictions, remove another sticky note and ask students to readjust their predictions. Will their final number still work or have they changed their idea of what the pattern might be? Again, have each child record their prediction and then have them share with the class or with a partner. Continue to remove sticky notes and discuss predictions until the pattern is revealed.

Tip: Support struggling students by providing them with hundred charts to use as a visual as they think about possible patterns.

Questions for Discussion

1. How does an understanding of patterns help students better understand place value and operations?

2. How can an understanding of patterns help students solve problems?

3. How might teachers support students who have trouble recognizing patterns?

4. In what ways can an understanding of patterns support students who are struggling with basic math facts?

CHAPTER 6

Strategy

Make a Table

Organizing data in a table is an essential mathematical skill. It helps children to see relationships within patterns and eventually to generalize these relationships to form a rule.

—Terrence G. Coburn

The ability to organize data so that it can be used to solve problems is a critical skill. Tables are one way in which students can organize data in order to see the data more clearly, recognize patterns and relationships within the data, and gain insights about missing data. When making tables, students are challenged to put important problem data in an organized form.

When focusing on the development of this strategy, there are several critical points to address. Students need to understand how to create a table, including which items to list on the table, where to record specific data on the table, how to determine when enough information has been gathered to complete the table, and even how to select the correct answer from the many numbers that are recorded on the table. Students must acquire the skill of recognizing and extending patterns and identifying functional relationships in order to construct and interpret tables accurately. And of course, recognizing whether creating a table makes sense for a problem is a critical skill. Spending time addressing each of these issues ensures that students have a solid understanding of this strategy.

Using Tables to Solve Problems

Tables are helpful in showing relationships between data. Take the following data, for example: *At the grocery store, each box of cereal costs $2.50.* A table like the one that follows can help students find out the cost for 2, 3, 4, or 5 boxes of cereal. In this problem, there is a relationship—a connection—between the cost of the cereal and the number of boxes, and the table shows that relationship. Every box of cereal costs $2.50, so each time a box of cereal is added to the top row of the table, $2.50 must be added to the corresponding column on the bottom row. By creating a table, students are able to get a better look at the data, use patterns to explore the data, and use the data to solve problems.

Number of boxes	1	2	3	4	5
Cost of cereal	$2.50	$5.00	$7.50	$10.00	$12.50

An important understanding for effectively using tables as a problem-solving strategy is identifying why and in what situations creating a table would make sense to help us find solutions. A critical insight in deciding if a table might be an appropriate strategy is recognizing two (or more) items in the problem that have a relationship or a connection, meaning that one item is connected to the other in a predictable way. Teacher modeling, through think-alouds, is an effective way to start discussions and exploration of the appropriate use of tables as a problem-solving strategy. Take the following problem:

Five people can fit in 1 car. If there are 20 people, how many cars will we need?

What do we already know? There is a relationship, a connection, between the number of people and number of cars. Can we figure out how many people can ride in 2 cars based on what we know? How about 3 cars? If I have 1 car, then I can fit 5 people in it. So, if I have 2 cars, then I can fit [5 + 5] or 10 people. If I have 3 cars, I can fit [5 + 5 + 5] or 15 people, and so on. How can we display that data so we can see it more clearly? How about a table on which we can record the data as we figure it out? Talking students through the creation of the table, including discussions about our thinking and the decisions we make as we move toward a solution, are valuable ways to help students develop their skills with this strategy.

To help students develop this skill, we might ask them to read a problem and underline the data that are connected.

To make <u>1 cake</u> I need <u>3 eggs</u>. How many eggs do I need to make 4 cakes? *(One cake and 3 eggs are connected because I need 3 eggs for every 1 cake.)*

<u>One loaf of bread</u> costs <u>$2.79</u>. How much do 6 loaves of bread cost? *(One loaf of bread and $2.79 are connected because I need $2.79 for each loaf of bread.)*

Once students begin to recognize the data that are connected, we can demonstrate how to create a table with those items. Have pairs or groups of students practice setting up tables from a series of problems. Working with a partner or team will allow students to hear one another's ideas and will help them learn to recognize that when they see a relationship between items in a problem, the creation of a table will be an effective way to organize that data so they can see it more clearly.

Once students are able to recognize a table problem and set up the rows, labeled with each item name, students must use the known data to help them complete the remainder of the table. Consider the previous cake problem. Initially, you may need to talk students through each step to determine how many eggs are needed to make 4 cakes. As students think through the problem, "1 cake uses 3 eggs, so 2 cakes use 6 eggs," the data can be recorded on the table. Demonstrating by constructing a table on the blackboard or overhead projector as students talk through the missing data will help them visualize the process.

Number of cakes	1	2
Number of eggs	3	6

We often provide primary students with tables that are already constructed and ask them to simply fill in some missing data. Intermediate students, however, should be given opportunities to create their own tables once they understand how to construct a table to represent data from a problem. It is important to share tables that are both horizontal and vertical. The positioning of the table is not important; it is the organized placement of the data that is important. Show students that the same data can be represented in different ways as long as the data is organized. Modeling some examples for the class while thinking aloud about which data are connected, how to organize the data on a table, and why a table might be helpful will provide students with opportunities to hear valuable thinking.

Recognizing Patterns and Functions

Although initially students will complete the "Number of eggs" row in the previous problem by adding 3 eggs each time they add another cake, many will quickly recognize the pattern appearing in the row and simply continue to fill in the numbers as they "count by threes." This recognition of the pattern is an important insight for students and illustrates the power of tables to organize data so that patterns emerge. Sharing observations about patterns will help students recognize the importance of finding a pattern in order to complete tables and, ultimately, solve problems.

Although students may initially see this as a pattern of adding 3, multiples of 3, or skip counting by 3, observation and discussion will lead them to discover another relationship between the numbers on the table. Rather than looking horizontally at the patterns that are created, students might notice that when they look at the vertical columns there is a relationship there, too. Students might observe that the number of eggs is always three times the number of cakes. This relationship, that explains the change that is occurring, is called a *function*. As students better understand functions they are able to solve more complex problems. What if I wanted to bake 50 cakes? Knowing the functional relationship of 3 eggs for every 1 cake allows students to determine that they will need 150 eggs (3 eggs × 50 cakes). The understanding of functions is critical to the study of algebra, and practice with tables will help strengthen this skill. Having students describe the functional relationship in algebraic terms (e.g., $3 \times c = e$, where c = number of cakes and e = number of eggs) is a great introduction to important algebra skills.

Selecting the Correct Answer

A final stumbling block for students in solving problems by making tables comes after the table is created. Many students are quick to recognize the relationship and create the table but have a difficult time choosing the correct answer from the many numbers recorded on the table. This is a critical step, since the creation of the table alone does not solve the problem—it only provides the data from which the problem can be solved. Discussions and demonstrations about how to locate the answer among all of the values on the table are essential.

Locating the answer from the data on a table begins with locating the "known" data, which then leads students to the "unknown" data. First, ask students to go back to the question: How many eggs do we need for 4 cakes? Have them locate 4 cakes on their table and then look for the quantity of eggs that corresponds to that number of cakes. It will be in the same column, directly above or below the 4 cakes on a horizontal table, or will be in the same row, next to the 4 cakes on a vertical table. Teachers might work with a table on an overhead projector or blackboard and place their finger on the number 4 and then move their finger directly up or down on the chart to find the matching answer, reminding students that rereading the question to find the "known" information is a key to figuring out where to look for the "unknown" information.

Number of cakes	1	2	3	4
Number of eggs	3	6	9	⑫

Number of cakes	Number of eggs
1	3
2	6
3	9
4	⑫

Solving More Sophisticated Table Problems

In the intermediate grades, table problems become more complex. In some cases, the answer to the problem does not appear on the table itself. Consider the following problem:

> **If you are purchasing cupcakes at $0.69 each, how many cupcakes can you buy for $3.00?**

Although $3.00 will not appear on the table, viewing a completed table will help students determine the appropriate answer. When looking at a table like the one that follows, students will see that they will be able to afford 4 cupcakes, but do not have enough money for 5.

Number of cupcakes	1	2	3	4	5
Cost	$0.69	$1.38	$2.07	$2.76	$3.45

More sophisticated problems may require tables that have more than two rows or columns, like the following:

For the math activity, each student needed 1 ruler, 3 strips of paper, and 4 paper clips. How many rulers, strips of paper, and paper clips were needed for a group of 6 students?

There is a relationship between three items, which is represented on the following table.

Number of rulers	1	2	3	4	5	6
Number of strips of paper	3	6	9	12	15	18
Number of paper clips	8	12	16	20	24	28

Challenging students with problems that include more complicated data, like fractions or decimals, integrates problem-solving practice with computational practice. And providing opportunities for students to apply their understanding of tables as they solve problems in geometry will extend their skills in the use of the strategy. Students might be asked to construct rows of connected squares using toothpicks and then to explore the connection between the number of squares in the row and the number of toothpicks used. Their understanding of tables will allow them to organize the data, discover relationships between the data, and solve more complex versions of the problem (i.e., How many toothpicks would be needed to make a row of 50 connected squares?).

Squares	1	2	3	4
Toothpicks	4	7	10	13

By constructing a table, students will gain insight into the relationships between the data and recognize that the initial square requires 4 toothpicks, but each additional square in the row only requires an additional 3 toothpicks. This pattern helps them extend the data even if they do not have enough toothpicks to actually form the rows of squares. And the insight that there is a functional relationship ($3x + 1$ or triple the number of squares and add 1 more to get the number of toothpicks) will allow students to quickly find the number of toothpicks needed to construct a row of 20 squares or 50 squares or 100 squares. The goal is to continue to challenge students with problems that push their thinking and to help them know that they have the foundational skills to tackle the more complex tasks. Always ask questions to ensure that students are looking at both patterns and functions and provide them with frequent opportunities to discuss the values they see on the table, especially when using more complicated data.

Using Tables to Connect to Other Math Skills

Students begin using tables to organize data and observe relationships between the data. Insights about their tables and the data on the tables often lead them to insights about other math concepts and alternate ways of finding solutions. After discussing the table that folllows, which shows the number of tickets needed to buy cookies at the carnival bake sale, fifth graders made the following comments as they discussed how they knew that 15 belonged in the blank space on the table:

Tickets	2	4	6	8	10
Cookies	3	6	9	12	

"It's fifteen because you add 3 more and 12 + 3 = 15." (Notice the recognition of patterns.)

"You could just multiply 5 × 3 because the bottom row is all multiples of three like 1 × 3 and 2 × 3 and 3 × 3 and 4 × 3, so the next one is 5 × 3." (Notice the recognition of multiples.)

"Hey, it's like equivalent fractions because $\frac{2}{3}$ is the same as $\frac{4}{6}$ and $\frac{6}{9}$ and $\frac{8}{12}$, so $\frac{10}{15}$ is the same as $\frac{2}{3}$, too." (Notice the understanding of equivalent fractions.)

"To find the number on the bottom, you take the number on the top and add $\frac{1}{2}$ to it, like 10 + half of ten (5) is 15, so 15 belongs on the bottom. The bottom number is always the top number plus another half of the top number." (Notice the recognition of a functional relationship.)

"I don't think you even need all the numbers in between because you could just say $\frac{2}{3}$ and $\frac{10}{15}$ are the same because you multiply the numerator and denominator by 5." (Notice the transition to proportions.)

Note: Horizontal tables are particularly effective for insights about fractions and proportions because the data is entered in a similar format.

Creating and exploring tables will lead students to insights about other efficient ways to solve problems including multiplication, proportions, and equivalent fractions. The goal is for students to have a greater repertoire of approaches for solving problems and a better understanding of the math they use to get to solutions. Frequently ask students to explain their insights as they search for patterns and functions and encourage them to discover alternate ways to find answers to problems.

Deciding When to Use a Table

With practice, students will become proficient at creating tables, but the ability to construct a table is only a part of the skills needed. Assisting students in developing the reasoning skill of deciding when this strategy should be used is critical to making it an effective problem-solving tool. After reading a problem that might lend itself to a table, ask students if the problem reminds them of any others they have seen. You might ask them if there is any data that is connected, that when one part changes so does the other. That insight indicates that a table might be an effective way to record and organize the data for further analysis. Asking students to justify their choice of strategies will help you see if they've truly mastered not only the mechanics of the skill but the concept of when it is best used and how it helps them better view and analyze data.

A Look at Student Work

In analyzing students' writing, we can see the development of their understanding of tables from a very basic level to a more sophisticated understanding. While tables are initially seen as simple forms on which data is recorded, opportunities for discussion and reflection lead students to discover the value of tables for helping them better analyze data to find solutions to problems.

Third-grade students used toothpicks to create rows of 2, 3, and 4 connected triangles and then began to gather data about the number of triangles in the row and the perimeter of the row of triangles that had been created. They were then challenged to determine the perimeter for a row of 20 triangles, even though they did not have enough toothpicks to actually create the row. Many students decided to record their data in tables. One student created a rather lengthy horizontal table showing the data for rows of 1 to 20 triangles and the related data showing the perimeters for each row.

Triangles	1	2	3	4	5	6	7	8	9	10	11	12	13	14	15	16	17	18	19	20
Perimeter	3	4	5	6	7	8	9	10	11	12	13	14	15	16	17	18	19	20	21	22

She wrote "First I made a table. Then I found the pattern for perimeter which is just 3, 4, 5, 6, and so on. Then I kept adding 1 to the pattern each time until I got to 20 triangles. The perimeter was 22."

Another student created a vertical table (see Figure 6–1), and although he found the same answer, had a different observation after viewing the data on his table. He discovered a functional relationship between the number of triangles and the perimeter recognizing that the perimeter would always be the number of triangles plus 2. Through later class sharing, the students were able to see each other's insights.

An important understanding in the use of tables is that data must be collected *and then* analyzed. The student in Figure 6–2 quickly began her table with the pattern that she assumed would appear on the table. After some questions by the teacher designed to redirect her to the data, she realized that the data was not accurately reflecting the problem and began again. Notice that the student placed her first effort in brackets rather than erasing it, a technique that helps teachers better see the development of students' thinking as they work through problems. Her writing at the conclusion of the task indicates that she understood how to locate answers from her revised table.

In Figure 6–3, the data was complicated by the inclusion of fractions, as well as missing numbers within the table. The student needed to use his understanding of tables and patterns to determine the missing data. The student's writing demonstrated his understanding of the data as he justified his answers.

Having students share their varied approaches to solving problems can lead to productive class discussions. While some students used diagrams and operations to

A Row of Triangles

With one triangle, the perimeter is 3 units. With a row of 2
connected triangles, the perimeter is 4 units.

What is the perimeter for a row of 20 triangles? ___22___

Triangles	Perimeter
1 +2 =	3
2 +2 =	4
3 +2 =	5
4 +2 =	6
5 +2 =	7
6	8
7	9
8	10

Explain how you solved this problem.

*I know it is 22 because 20+2=22 because
the perimeter are adding 2 to the
triangles.*

Figure 6–1 *This student displayed the data in a vertical table and observed a
functional relationship between the triangles and perimeters.*

solve a class problem, the student in Figure 6–4 shared the table she created to effectively solve it. A well-facilitated class discussion helped students recognize the appropriateness of various strategies.

Communicating About the Strategy

Asking students to write about and talk about using tables is a great way to assess
students' understanding of this strategy. Try prompts like:

- Explain how making a table helped you find the answer.
- Explain how you know which number on the table is the answer to the problem.
- Explain how you know which two (or more) items in the problem should be
  used to create your table.
- Describe the patterns you see on your table.

The Bake Sale

Erica was helping her mom make some cakes for the school bake sale. For each cake, Erica needed 3 eggs and 2 cups of flour. If Erica used 12 eggs, how many cups of flour did she use?

8 cups of flour

| [ea.] eggs | 3 | 4 | 5 | 6 | 7 | 8 |
| cups of flour | 2 | 4 | 6 | 8 | 10 | 12 |

eggs	3	6	9	12	15	18
cups of flour	2	4	6	8	10	12
	1 cake	2 cakes	3 cakes	4 cakes	5 cakes	6 cakes

Explain how you could figure out the number of eggs they would need if they used 10 cups of flour.

You need 15 eggs if they used 10 cups of flour because you filled the [ea.] egg data by counting by 3's and the 15 is right above the 10.

Figure 6–2 *Brackets around this student's initial attempt at creating the table help us see how the table was revised.*

- Explain how you knew when you had enough data on your table to solve the problem.
- Why was making a table a good strategy for solving this problem?

A Note About Tables

Not all tables show patterns and functions. Some tables are simply data tables (e.g., a table showing the number of points each player scored in a basketball game or a table to show the cost of tickets for various airline trips). Tables or charts can be used to record a variety of information and may not always show patterns and functions. When we refer to making tables as a problem-solving strategy, however, we are generally referring to those tables that help us explore connected information through patterns and functions as a way of getting to a problem solution. Helping students also see that other data might be recorded on a table, and that data from those tables might be used to solve problems, are important insights in building students' understanding of tables as a tool to solve problems. I may need to know how many points each player scored in a basketball game in order to solve a problem asking me to determine the average points scored, but there is not a connection between the number

Shake It Up

Aidan was making strawberry milk shakes for his friends, but he spilled milk on the paper that showed the ingredients he should use and when he wiped off the paper some of the numbers disappeared. Help Aidan figure out the missing data and record it on the table below.

Number of shakes	1	2	3	4
Milk (cups)	$\frac{1}{2}$	1	$1\frac{1}{2}$	2
Sliced strawberries (cups)	1/3	2/3	1	$1\frac{1}{3}$
Ice cream (cups)	2/3	$1\frac{1}{3}$	2	2 2/3

1. Explain how you know how many cups of ice cream Aidan will need to make two milk shakes.

I Know how many cups of ice cream Aidan needs to make the milkshakes because there is a pattern. Each time it goes up by $\frac{2}{3}$. So $\frac{2}{3} + \frac{2}{3} = 1\frac{1}{3}$.   Answer = $1\frac{1}{3}$ cups of ice cream.

2. Explain how you know how many cups of strawberries Aidan will need to make four milk shakes.

I Know because there is a pattern. Each time it goes up by a $\frac{1}{3}$. So $1 + \frac{1}{3} = 1\frac{1}{3}$ Answer = $1\frac{1}{3}$ cups of strawberries

Figure 6–3 *Fractions complicate the data on this table, but this student explains how he found the missing data.*

of points scored by each player that allows me to use patterns or functions to complete that table. The data table simply provides me with the necessary information to solve the problem. Teachers might ask students to look at a table and determine if it has patterns and functions or is simply a data table. Recognizing the difference between these types of tables will avoid misunderstandings for your students.

C L A S S R O O M - T E S T E D   T I P

Guess My Rule

Use In/Out Tables as a quick warm-up activity to help students explore tables and share their insights about the patterns and functions they see. Put a blank table, like the one that follows, on the blackboard, overhead projector, or on chart paper. Begin to fill in a value in the "In" column and then place a value

Figure 6–4 *This student records her way of solving a problem as the class discusses possible strategies.*

in the "Out" column, challenging students to come up with the rule to explain how the "Out" value was determined. Do a few examples and then ask students to turn and share their ideas with a partner to engage all students in discussion about what they are observing. Pairs might be asked to share what they believe is the rule. Help students build algebraic thinking by challenging them to express the rule using the language of algebra. Rather than saying you added 2 to each number, students might begin to express it as "$n + 2$." Vary this activity by asking students to work with a partner to develop a rule and then see if the class can guess their rule.

IN	OUT
4	1
6	3
8	5
n	$n - 3$

CLASSROOM-TESTED TIP

Using Recipe Data in Tables

Recipes provide the perfect real data to explore tables. Select a recipe with data (whole numbers or fractions) that work for the level of your students. Tell students that you are going to continue to increase the recipe so it will feed more people. Have them construct tables to show the data as it is increased. Or to stimulate quick but thoughtful discussions, challenge students by providing them with a table with missing data like the example that follows. Ask students to decide what is missing and explain how they know what the missing values should be. Ask questions to ensure that students are looking at both patterns and functions on the table.

BANANA SMOOTHIE

Cups of milk	1	2	3	4
Cups of mashed ripe banana	½	1		2
Cups of chocolate syrup	⅓	⅔	1	

Questions for Discussion

1. How can attention to the Make a Table strategy help your students learn to organize information? What can you do to ensure that your students recognize that the organization of data is a key for this strategy?

2. How might you simplify this strategy for students who are at a beginning level in their understanding?

3. How might you continue to challenge students who are successfully using tables as a problem-solving tool?

4. In what ways might working with tables reinforce your students' skills and concepts related to basic operations, fractions, and decimals?

Strategy

Make an Organized List

Through group and classroom discussions, students can examine a variety of approaches and learn to evaluate appropriate strategies for a given solution.

—National Council of Teachers of Mathematics,
Curriculum and Evaluation Standards for School Mathematics

In the previous chapter, we discussed the importance of students organizing problem data to find a solution. While tables provide one way to organize data when there are connections between and among the data, this chapter will explore another way to organize data—the use of an organized list. Making an organized list is a valuable strategy when students are faced with problems that require determining all the possible combinations for a given situation. Students might be exploring all the possible double-dip ice cream cone combinations that can be made using vanilla, chocolate, and strawberry ice cream or the number of possible drink/snack combinations that can be made from milk, cola, lemonade, cookies, popcorn, and peanuts. Students who are able to record and organize data in a systematic way are better able to keep track of the data and determine all of the possibilities.

Organize and Record

The two words describing this strategy—*organized list*—pinpoint the key ideas for the strategy.

1. *List* ideas, or get them out of your head and onto paper, so you will remember them.

2. Proceed in an *organized* way so you will know what has already been considered and can ensure that no possibilities have been missed.

Recording and organizing information are critical to effective problem solving and yet many students do not intuitively do either when they are faced with a problem. When attempting to figure out all the possible combinations of shirts (blue, red, and green) and shorts (black and brown), students often randomly recite possibilities. As students proceed in a random fashion, they become confused and unsure of which combinations have already been given or which combinations have been missed altogether. Teaching students to find a starting point, to begin with one item and then exhaust all possible combinations with that item before moving on to another item, will help them proceed in an organized manner and recognize when they have listed all of the possibilities. And by recording each possibility, students learn to simplify the task as they are able to keep track of their ideas and double-check their thinking.

> blue shirt—black pants
> blue shirt—brown pants
>
> *Those are the only pants, so I'm done with the blue shirt. I'll try the red shirt next.*
>
> red shirt—black pants
> red shirt—brown pants
>
> *Now I'm done with the red shirt. I'll try the green shirt.*
>
> green shirt—black pants
> green shirt—brown pants
>
> *I have no more shirts, so I must be done!*

Hands-on introductory activities help students experiment with this strategy. In early experiences, students might use color tiles to represent various shirt or pant color combinations, trying the different combinations and then recording each one. Or students might use paper cutouts to represent three different race cars and physically experiment with the possible order of their finish in a race (see Car Template on the CD). While students try the different combinations with hands-on materials, encourage them to find an organized way of proceeding and to record the combinations they have tried. Have them share their approaches with each other and discuss the different ways in which they chose to record their combinations. In the intermediate grades, students transition from recording their ideas on simple lists to the use of more complicated lists or tree diagrams to record the problem information. As students gain confidence with the strategy, continue to challenge them with more difficult problems.

Laying the Foundation for More Sophisticated Skills

Organized list problems can begin quite simply. In simple combination problems, a goal is to help students understand the importance of finding a starting point and exhausting all possibilities before moving on. Consider the following problem:

> **Jill had ice cream for dessert. She could have one scoop of either chocolate, strawberry, or vanilla ice cream. She could have it in a cone or a cup. What are the different possibilities for Jill's dessert?**

Third-grade students attempted to find all of the possible dessert combinations with the three flavors and either a cone or cup. Ali said "I started with the chocolate ice cream and put it with a cone and a cup, then strawberry with a cone and a cup, then vanilla with both. That was all the ice cream so I got six ways and I was done." Ali recognized that she must have gotten all of the possibilities because she did it in an organized way and knew that she found each combination. Ali's choice of beginning with chocolate ice cream was a good one, since it is first in the list of flavors, but even if she had started with the last flavor of ice cream, as long as she moved in an organized manner so she could keep track of what had already been done, she would have been able to find the solution.

Once students have internalized the skill of moving through data in an organized way, helping them explore alternate ways to record their ideas will help them further develop their skills and prepare them for the more sophisticated problems they will face. Students begin to recognize that using initials or symbols might be more efficient than writing entire words on a list and so chocolate becomes *c*, strawberry becomes *s*, and vanilla becomes *v*. And tree diagrams become a new way to help students organize their data. The thinking skill of beginning with one item, and exhausting possibilities before moving on to another item, is central to the concept of a tree diagram. A tree diagram is another way to help students organize the data as they move through each possibility as in this diagram:

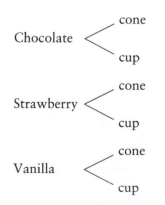

The understanding of organized thinking and the ability to use a tree diagram will support students as they explore problems like the following:

Peggy had an ice cream sundae for dessert. She could have chocolate, strawberry, or vanilla ice cream. She could add hot fudge, marshmallow, or caramel sauce. She could top it off with whipped cream or no topping at all. What are the different sundaes that Peggy might have for dessert?

With the additional data, the problem becomes more confusing. Students who randomly guess possibilities will have a difficult time keeping the data straight without repeating or forgetting possibilities. And recording in a list format requires them to repeatedly write the same words, a lengthy process. Their ability to diagram the possibilities helps to simplify and shorten this otherwise confusing and lengthy task.

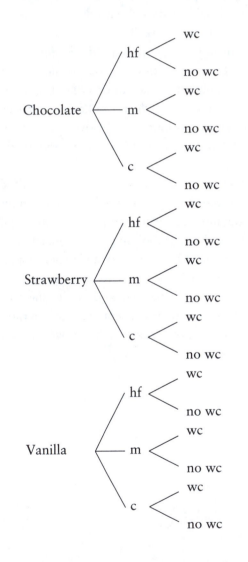

And combination problems can become even more complicated. Students might be asked to find all of the coin combinations they could use to pay for a pretzel with exact change if the pretzel costs $0.25. There are many possible combinations in this

problem and many opportunities to become confused. An organized way of recording the data becomes essential. Students can use lessons learned through their experiences with simpler problems to find a starting point, move in a systematic way, and
record data in order to keep track of their thinking.

Quarters	Dimes	Nickels	Pennies
1	0	0	0
0	2	1	0
0	2	0	5
0	1	3	0
0	1	2	5
0	1	1	10
0	1	0	15
0	0	5	0
0	0	4	5
0	0	3	10
0	0	2	15
0	0	1	20
0	0	0	25

By proceeding in an organized manner, students are able to determine all of the
possibilities. And insights about patterns arise as students notice the patterns in the
numbers recorded on their lists. Terri remarked, "Look at the patterns in the pennies
column! I didn't even have to really think about it—I knew which number would
come next!" Patterns will emerge to help simplify the problem for those students who
record their data in an organized way, not for those who randomly list possibilities.

And what if a problem asks for the possible combinations that could be used to
buy a soda for $0.50 cents if the soda machine will only accept quarters, dimes, and
nickels? Finding a way to begin (say with the largest possible coin) and exhausting
all of the possibilities (and recording each one) before moving to the next coin is of
critical importance to simplify these more difficult tasks. As the complexity of problems increases, our students benefit from the foundation skills they have developed
through their experiences with simpler problems.

Combinations Versus Permutations

The previous ice cream problems are examples of combination problems. In combination problems, the order does not matter. Chocolate ice cream and a cone is the same
as a cone and chocolate ice cream. They are not two different dessert possibilities. The
organized list strategy also supports students with permutation problems. In permutation problems, order matters. If Ty is going to the fair and will ride the roller coaster,

scrambler, and ferris wheel and we want to figure out all of the different orders in which he might ride the three rides, we find he could ride the roller coaster first, the scrambler second, and the ferris wheel third. Even though it is the same three rides, a different possibility would be to ride the scrambler first, the ferris wheel second, and the roller coaster third. While these problems are a bit different than combination problems, the organized list strategy will support students to simplify the somewhat confusing task. Again, beginning with one ride and exhausting all possibilities with that ride first, before moving to the next ride, would be a good plan to stay on track.

> roller coaster, scrambler, ferris wheel
> roller coaster, ferris wheel, scrambler
> *There are no other ways to do it with riding the roller coaster first. So let's ride the scrambler first.*

> scrambler, roller coaster, ferris wheel
> scrambler, ferris wheel, roller coaster
> *Now, we're done with options for riding the scrambler first, so how about riding the ferris wheel first?*

> ferris wheel, roller coaster, scrambler
> ferris wheel, scrambler, roller coaster
> *There are no more rides, so those must be the only options!*

Formulas and Organized Lists

As students work on organized lists, they develop the groundwork for more sophisticated mathematical skills including mathematical formulas that may help them arrive at answers when data becomes challenging. Consider the problem in which students need to determine the number of shirt/short combinations possible with 2 shirts (blue and green) and 3 shorts (red, yellow, and black). It doesn't matter whether the student records a blue shirt with red shorts or red shorts with a blue shirt; regardless of the order in which they are recorded, the combinations are the same. As students work on similar combination problems, they often notice a formula—if there are x of one item and y of another item, then there are xy possibilities. Students will discover that 2 shirts and 3 shorts will yield 2×3 or 6 possible combinations. They have discovered the formula for finding the number of combinations!

In permutation problems, the order is a critical element in determining the number of combinations. Consider the problem in which students are asked to find the number of possible three-digit numbers that could be created by arranging, but not repeating, the digits 1, 2, and 3. The number 123 is different from 132, which is different from 231. Each ordered group is a different possibility. As students work on similar permutation problems, they develop skills in *factorials*. They may discover that three digits can be arranged in $3 \times 2 \times 1$ ways or 6 ways. While this concept is generally taught in the middle grades, intermediate students often discover the formula as they record, observe, and discuss their findings. Good problem solvers are constantly observant and look for short cuts (or formulas) based on their observations!

When first experimenting with formulas, students may continue to use lists to verify their answers and test to be sure that the formulas will yield the correct results. Miguel said, "I think the answer will be 10 because there are 2 shirts and 5 pants, and yesterday we had 3 drinks and 3 kinds of pizzas and got 9 possibilities, so I think we just do 2×5 to get the answer." Miguel's hypothesis was built on observations of previous problems, but he continued to create organized lists to check his thinking until convinced that his formula would work. Predicting and testing ideas is a strong way for students to explore, understand, and retain mathematical formulas.

Formulas can provide a shortcut for solving problems, but are not always the best approach. In the problem in Figure 7–1, students are asked to determine how

Lunch Choices

Jennifer wants to order a sandwich and a drink. Look at the menu below to decide how many different choices she has.

LUNCH MENU

<u>SANDWICHES</u>
Chicken
Ham
Tuna

<u>DRINKS</u>
Lemonade
Milk

CL
CM
HL
HM
TL
TM

There are 6 diffrent ways.

How did making an organized list help you solve this problem?

Making a organized list helped me solved this problem by helping me keep things in order and helping me by not writing something twice.

Figure 7–1 *This student decides to use initials for each sandwich and drink. Her writing shows that she understands the value of organized lists.*

many combinations are possible for 3 types of sandwiches and 2 types of drinks. Students might make an organized list or use a formula to find the number of choices possible. However, if there were 7 kinds of sandwiches and 9 kinds of drinks, it would be helpful to know the formula since a list of 63 possibilities would be quite lengthy to construct! The formula allows us to determine the answer even when the data gets lengthy and complicated. But a formula is not always the best route to an answer. What if the question had not asked for the number of possibilites, but rather asked the student to list the possible combinations? Now, the formula does not lead us to the answer. Or if the problem had listed the prices for each sandwich and each drink and then asked which sandwich/drink combinations Joe could buy if he had $2.75 (or some other designated amount of money), the formula would not allow us to take all of the data into consideration. The new question is not asking how many combinations are possible, but is asking which combinations fit a certain set of criteria. To solve that problem, students need to determine the possible combinations and then do the computations to see which would work for Joe. Both organized thinking and the use of formulas help us solve problems. Students who have facility with both, and understand when each one makes sense, are more likely to find solutions to the varied problems they might face.

A Look at Student Work

Primary students often draw objects as they try to determine combinations, but students in grades 3 through 5 discover that representing the items in lists can be quicker and easier. Students may begin lists by recording the entire word, but soon see that initials or abbreviations work well and save time (refer back to Figure 7–1). Share the varied ways that students represent items on their lists. It is the organization of the items that is most important, not the words or initials that are selected to represent those items. The student writing in Figure 7–1 illustrates an understanding of the value of organizing items on a list.

Tree diagrams are an effective way to represent combinations. Although these are technically diagrams rather than lists, they are discussed in this chapter because of their ability to assist with combination problems. It is important to demonstrate for students how to create these diagrams to represent the data and how to count the final column to get the total number of possible combinations. The foundation for effectively using a tree diagram is the ability to organize data by beginning with one item and then exhausting all of the possibilities before moving on to the next item (the same thinking skill that is critical for making organized lists). It is simply the way of recording the data that differs. Students who have learned how to create organized lists will move quickly into the skill of creating tree diagrams, using their knowledge of finding a starting point and then working systematically through the data and exhausting all possibilities before moving on to the next piece of data. In the work sample in Figure 7–2, a student shares his tips for creating a tree diagram and illustrates an understanding of this process.

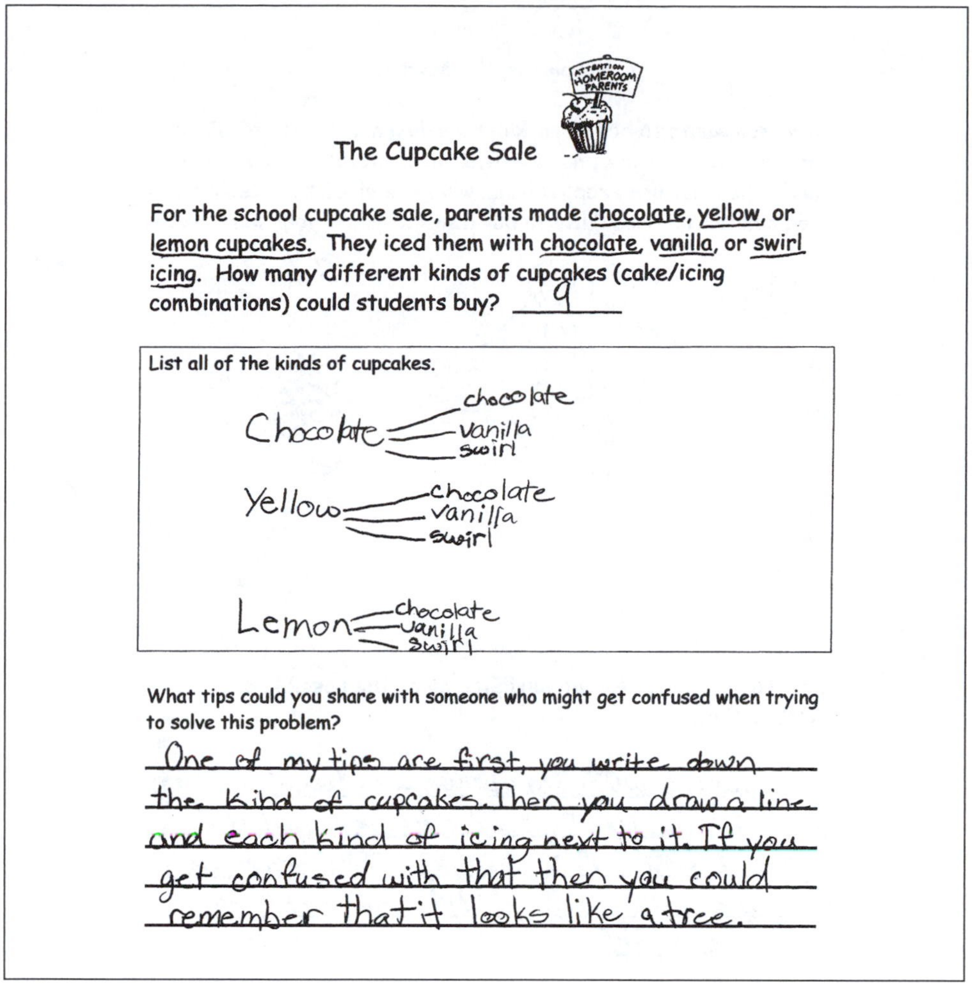

The Cupcake Sale

For the school cupcake sale, parents made <u>chocolate</u>, <u>yellow</u>, or <u>lemon cupcakes.</u> They iced them with <u>chocolate</u>, <u>vanilla</u>, or <u>swirl</u> <u>icing</u>. How many different kinds of cupcakes (cake/icing combinations) could students buy? ____9____

List all of the kinds of cupcakes.

Chocolate — chocolate / vanilla / swirl

Yellow — chocolate / vanilla / swirl

Lemon — chocolate / vanilla / swirl

What tips could you share with someone who might get confused when trying to solve this problem?

One of my tips are first, you write down the kind of cupcakes. Then you draw a line and each kind of icing next to it. If you get confused with that then you could remember that it looks like a tree.

Figure 7–2 *Asking students to share tips for a strategy is a good way of checking their understanding.*

As problems become increasingly complex, it is critical that students can find a way to organize the data in order to simplify the problem. In Figures 7–3 and 7–4, fifth-grade students chose different methods for recording their thinking, but each student used a systematic approach for moving through the possibilities. The student in Figure 7–3 chose to diagram the data, while the student in Figure 7–4 created a table to record the problem information. In each case, their representations and writing show their understanding of the strategy.

Remind students that a list or tree diagram is not the answer to a problem, it is a strategy to help them arrive at the answer. The problem may be asking how many combinations are possible, which combination the student would choose, or which combinations satisfy certain criteria. The lists and diagrams are tools to help students find the answer.

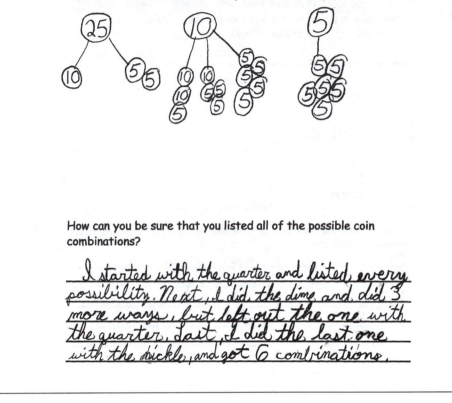

Coins in the Machine

Jackson wants to buy a snack in a vending machine that will take only quarters, dimes, and nickels. If each snack costs 35 cents, and if he must use exact change, what are all of the possible coin combinations he could use to buy a snack? Show your work below.

How can you be sure that you listed all of the possible coin combinations?

I started with the quarter and listed every possibility. Next, I did the dime and did 3 more ways, but left out the one with the quarter. Last, I did the last one with the nickle, and got 6 combinations.

Figure 7–3 *This student chose to diagram the data, moving in an organized fashion from largest coin to smallest coin.*

Communicating About the Strategy

Don't forget to have students write about and talk about their strategy for solving the problem. Try prompts like:

- Explain why it's important to be organized when making your list.

- How did making a list help you solve this problem?

- Why is it important to record your combinations?

- How are tree diagrams and organized lists alike? How are they different?

- Are you sure there are no other possible combinations? Why?

- Why was making a list a good strategy for solving this problem?

- Is there a way to solve this problem other than making a list? Explain.

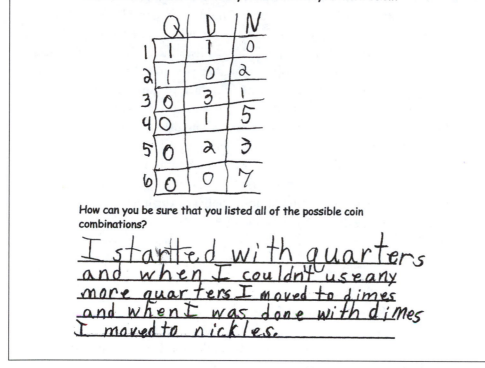

Coins in the Machine

Jackson wants to buy a snack in a vending machine that will take only quarters, dimes, and nickels. If each snack costs 35 cents, and if he must use exact change, what are all of the possible coin combinations he could use to buy a snack? Show your work below.

	Q	D	N
1	1	1	0
2	1	0	2
3	0	3	1
4	0	1	5
5	0	2	3
6	0	0	7

How can you be sure that you listed all of the possible coin combinations?

I started with quarters and when I couldn't use any more quarters I moved to dimes and when I was done with dimes I moved to nickles.

Figure 7–4 *This student created an organized data table to record the problem information.*

C L A S S R O O M - T E S T E D   T I P

Demonstrating the Need for Organization

Try a demonstration with three students in your class. Ask them to get in a line to sharpen their pencils. Create the line in front of the class, for example, Katie, then Colleen, then Erica. Ask the class how many other ways they might line up. As students in the class suggest other ways in which to order the three students, switch their order in the line. After a while, ask students "Is that all the possible ways? How many ways were there? Are you sure we've tried them all? Are you sure we haven't repeated any?" Ask students to talk with a partner and see if they can figure out a way to be sure that you have all the possible orders and haven't repeated any. You might prompt them with questions such as "How many ways can they line up if Katie is first? If Colleen is first? If Erica is first?" Students may come up with the idea of writing down each possibility, or they may even come up with an organized method to be sure they don't miss any possibilities. Praise their logical thinking as they share their ideas. Begin again, this time keeping an organized list.

Looking for Formulas

Guide students to a discovery of the formula for determining the number of combinations. Have students work in groups to solve a combination problem with their organized lists (try the Special Cookie Deals problems on the CD). Change the data for each group (i.e., one group might have a list of 3 cookies and 3 drinks, while another group will have a list of 2 cookies and 4 drinks). After each group solves their problem, reorganize the students into new groups of four so they are able to share their data from their original problem with new group members. Have them compile and record their data (number of cookies, number of drinks, number of possibilities) and discuss their observations. Students will begin to observe that 2 cookies and 4 drinks was (2×4) 8 possibilities, while 2 cookies and 3 drinks was (2×3) 6 possibilities and 3 cookies and 4 drinks was (3×4) 12 possibilities. Ask them to come up with a rule (formula) for finding the number of combinations. Challenge them to stay observant to see if their formula will always work!

Questions for Discussion

1. Why is it important for teachers to think aloud while demonstrating this problem-solving strategy?

2. What are *combinations*? What are *permutations*? How are they alike and different?

3. How might you teach both the organized thinking skill and the formulas? How can you help students understand when each might be helpful?

4. How does using lists help students make complicated problems simpler? Is helping students find a way to make hard problems easier a goal of problem-solving instruction? Why?

CHAPTER 8

Strategy

Draw a Picture or Diagram

The act of representing encourages children to focus on the essential characteristics of a situation.

—National Council of Teachers of Mathematics,
Curriculum and Evaluation Standards for School Mathematics

The old adage, "A picture is worth a thousand words," can be true in problem solving. Constructing a picture or diagram helps students visualize the problem. In problem solving, we encourage students to get problems out of their heads and make them visual. For primary students, we begin by acting out problem situations as we add candy to a dish and then move to manipulatives (e.g., cubes or counters) to represent the candy, still allowing students to visualize the situation. Many students in grades 3 through 5 continue to benefit from acting out problems, using real objects, and using manipulatives to represent problem situations, but we also support students as they strengthen their skills at creating diagrams as pictorial representations of the problem. After reading a problem, students should be able to use the data to create a picture or diagram that represents the problem situation. Problems that initially appear complex often become easy to solve when students are able to draw or diagram them. Consider the following problem:

> **Susie is decorating a birthday cake for her sister. She decorated the top of the circular cake with a ring of 8 roses. In between each rose, she put 2 candles. How old is Susie's sister?**

While the data may be difficult to process in our heads, a simple diagram of the cake will allow us to see the placement of the candles and count them to reveal the age of

Susie's sister. The problem is immediately simplified by creating a picture of the data as in the student work in Figure 8–1.

A New Meaning for the Word *Picture*

In problem solving, pictures should not be works of art. Discourage students from adding unnecessary details to their pictures. Coloring the picture is unnecessary unless the colors represent the data. While Student B's work in Figure 8–1 indicates that the student found the correct answer, the picture is much more elaborate than is necessary. Students need to be reminded that a square can represent a house or a car—the picture does not need to be realistic. Students often spend so much time creating a detailed picture that they never end up solving the problem. Focus students on the problem-solving process.

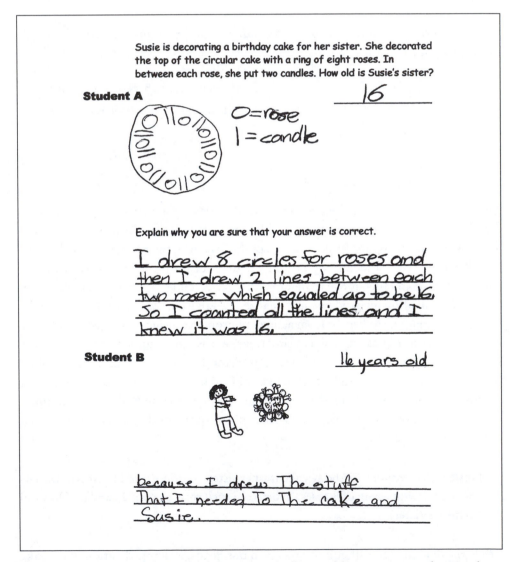

Figure 8–1 *Student A's simple diagram made this problem easier to solve. Student B was able to solve the problem, but the detailed picture was unnecessary.*

Simplifying Through Pictures

> There were 5 flags flying above the entrance to the amusement park. Each flag was flying at a different level. The red flag was flying higher than the green one. The yellow flag was lower than the green one. The purple flag was higher than the green one, but lower than the red one. The blue flag was a little lower than the yellow one. What was the order of flags from highest to lowest?

This type of problem often generates immediate anxiety because of the overload of information and confusing wording; however, if students are able to draw a picture or diagram to represent each piece of information, the problem becomes simple. A diagram serves to clarify the problem situation. It allows students to proceed one clue at a time, so it simplifies the task. By simply moving step by step and recording each color flag, students can proceed through the problem with ease.

First fact: **The red flag was flying higher than the green one.**

This fact is represented by the red flag being written above (indicating flying higher than) the green flag in the simple diagram.

Second fact: **The yellow flag was lower than the green one.**

red
green
yellow

If the yellow flag is flying lower then the green flag, that color is recorded below green in the diagram.

Third fact: **The purple flag was higher than the green one, but lower than the red one.**

red
purple
green
yellow

If the purple flag is higher than the green, but lower than the red, it will need to be recorded between those two colors.

Fourth fact: **The blue flag was a little lower than the yellow one.**

red
purple
green
yellow
blue

The blue flag is lower than the yellow, so it must be the lowest and the color is recorded at the bottom of the diagram.

Now the diagram is complete and not only can students clearly see the order of the flags, but there is a sense of accomplishment in solving this initially confusing problem. When asked what was hard about the problem, one fifth grader commented, "It was really confusing. It was hard to keep up with. I had to write it down." She then explained how she made the problem easier to solve by saying "When I first read it I couldn't understand. Then I drew a picture. That way you don't have to do all of it in your head." (*Note:* As students share approaches for solving this problem, a frequent insight is to leave spaces between items as they are recorded. Students report that it allows them to insert information at any place in their diagram. This insight shows the development of their skill with the strategy.)

Focusing on More Complex Problems

Initially, problems help students see the power of pictures and diagrams to simplify problems.

> The Boy Scouts were planning a breakfast in the school gym. There were 5 round tables and 4 square tables. 6 people can sit at each round table and 4 people can sit at each square table. How many people can sit at all of the tables?

Students can simply draw the tables, represent the boys at each table and count or add to find the solution. As students master representing data with pictures or diagrams, however, we challenge them with additional criteria. There is added complexity in this race car problem:

> There were 5 cars in the race. The blue car was in front of the green car. The yellow car was behind the green car. The red car was between the blue and green cars. The orange car was in front of the blue car. What was the order of the cars from first to last?

Students' confusion about order becomes apparent in this type of problem as they begin to represent the information and lose track of which car is "first" and which is "last." As students share their ways of recording the data, others will gain tips like recording "first" and "last" on their papers or drawing a finish line with cars lined up behind it.

| First | orange | blue | red | green | yellow | Last |

Discussing the parts of a problem that make it more challenging is an important component of the problem-solving experience.

Problems continue to gain complexity as in the following problem:

> I have 1 large bag. Inside the large bag are 2 medium bags. Inside each medium bag are 3 small bags. Inside each small bag are 3 tiny bags. Inside each tiny bag is a

quarter. How much money is in my bag? I plan to use the money in my bag to buy candy. Each piece of candy costs $0.20. How many pieces of candy can I buy?

This multistep problem could be simplified through a diagram to allow students to visualize the number of bags (and number of quarters). Students, however, will need to also use their understanding of money, as well as their computation skills, to find the solution. As problems get more complex, they push students to apply a variety of math skills.

James is helping his father fence in a part of the yard for a garden. The area they are fencing in is 20 feet wide and 16 feet long. They need to put a post in the ground every 4 feet. How many posts will they need?

To find a solution, students use their understanding of measurement and their computation skills, but are often jump-started by drawing the garden. The drawing allows them to visualize the problem situation, but is only the first step to finding the answer. As students experience success with simple problems, challenge them with problems that require them to merge their understanding of the strategy with other math skills (e.g., measurement, operations, fractions, decimals).

Differentiating Instruction Through Problem Solving

Often within the same classroom, students are at a variety of levels in their understanding and use of problem-solving strategies. Differentiating problems for varied groups within the classroom allows teachers to explore a similar strategy while supporting students with appropriate levels of problems. A third-grade teacher posed this problem to her class:

There were 20 children at the Valentine party. Each child could choose the flavor of sherbet he or she wanted for a snack. $\frac{1}{2}$ of the children chose orange sherbet $\frac{1}{5}$ of them chose lime. The others had raspberry. How many children had each kind of sherbet?

While some students were able to determine the amounts with their computation skills, many drew 20 items and circled $\frac{1}{2}$ or $\frac{1}{5}$ to see the numbers of students in each group. But, for one group in the class, the teacher posed a variation of the problem that was a bit more complex:

There were 20 children at the Valentine party. Each child could choose the flavor of sherbet he or she wanted for a snack. $\frac{1}{2}$ of the children chose orange sherbet. $\frac{1}{5}$ of the remaining children chose lime. Then, $\frac{1}{4}$ of the remaining children chose raspberry. The rest of the children had lemon. How many children had each kind of sherbet?

By adding additional data and the condition that it be the "remaining children," this problem challenged students beyond the original version of the problem. Adding layers of complexity to problems for specific students will keep them engaged and continue to push their thinking skills. Often simply changing the data to fractions, decimals, or percents serves to stimulate additional thinking.

Working in groups has many benefits in problem-solving instruction. It allows students to share ideas and hear each others' thinking. But students often work at different speeds, with some groups finishing while others are still actively engaged with the task. Teachers might consider posing a problem to all groups and asking groups to raise their hands as they finish the task. The teacher can then move to that group and ask them to explain or justify their answer in order to check their understanding. If students are ready to move on, the teacher might have a second-tier task ready to keep them involved in the activity. The bag and quarter problem above might be adapted to fit this instructional model.

> *Task 1*: **I have 1 large bag. Inside the large bag are 2 medium bags. Inside each medium bag are 3 small bags. Inside each small bag are 3 tiny bags. Inside each tiny bag is a quarter. How much money is in my bag?**

As groups complete the task, they raise their hands and the teacher joins their group. Group members justify their answers to the teacher and then a second part of the task is assigned.

> *Task 2*: **I plan to use the money in my bag to buy candy. Each piece of candy costs $0.20. How many pieces of candy can I buy?**

For the first part of the problem, students might draw a diagram to find the solution, but the second part requires using the answer to the first part along with an understanding of money and computational ability to find the amount of candy that can be bought. "What if" questions work well to extend thinking for groups who finish quickly. *What if* there were 2 large bags? *What if* there were 2 quarters in each tiny bag? *What if* the candy costs $0.25 a piece?

A Look at Student Work

For very young students, drawing pictures is an aid in helping them understand the simplest math concepts. As students learn to add 2 + 3, they draw pictures of two objects and three objects. This enables them to count their pictures to find the total. The picture helps to make the problem real and understandable. As students progress to the intermediate grades and their ability to work in the abstract increases, they no longer rely on pictures for many math concepts. There will, however, always be some problems that become more clear when a picture or diagram is used. In Figure 8–2, a student used a diagram to visualize the problem and then used an understanding of

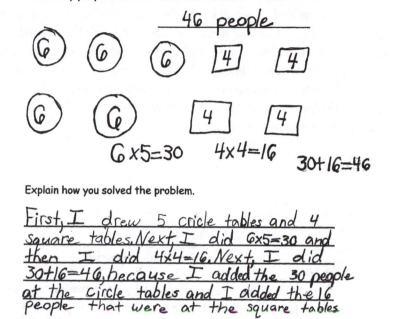

The Boy Scout Breakfast

The Boy Scouts were planning a breakfast in the school gym. There were <u>5 round tables</u> and <u>4 square tables</u>. <u>6 people can sit at each round table</u> and <u>4 people can sit at each square table.</u> How many people can sit at all of the tables?

<u>46 people</u>

6 x5=30   4x4=16   30+16=46

Explain how you solved the problem.

First, I drew 5 cricle tables and 4 square tables. Next I did 6x5=30 and then I did 4x4=16. Next, I did 30+16=46, because I added the 30 people at the circle tables and I added the 16 people that were at the square tables

Figure 8–2 *This student used both a picture and equations to find the solution to the problem.*

equations to work toward the solution. Students move to abstract representations at different rates. Sharing strategies and providing transitions by showing students how the picture led to the development of the equations will help to guide students as they transition to more abstract methods.

Some students are inclined to answer problems quickly, using just mental computations, rather than taking the time to draw diagrams of the problem. While that can be effective for some, it can also lead to errors. A simple picture often clarifies the problem and can illustrate an error in thinking. When asked to find the number of posts needed for the fence in the following problem, Jai made a mental error when solving it without the help of a visual.

James is helping his father fence in a part of the yard for a garden. The area they are fencing in is 20 feet wide and 16 feet long. They need to put a post in the ground every 4 feet. How many posts will they need?

Jai contended that he did not need to make a picture for the problem because he knew that there were "6 posts on the long sides because it is like 1 post and then another after 4 feet, 8 feet, 12 feet, 16 feet, and 20 feet," he said as he showed his thinking by counting the posts with his fingers as he spoke. "Then there are 5 posts on the shorter sides because you put a post and then one at 4, 8, 12, and 16 feet. So it is 6 + 6 + 5 + 5. You need 22 posts." A diagram would help Jai see that he needed only 18 posts, because his mental image did not allow him to visualize that some posts were shared posts at the corners and therefore did not need to be counted twice. For all students, a picture or diagram can be a great way to check for errors in thinking.

As students become more sophisticated, they find that diagrams are useful ways to illustrate problems for which solutions are not readily evident (see Figure 8–3). While the data in this problem initially appeared quite complex, the student was able to create a diagram to visualize the problem situation.

Figure 8–3 *This student was able to diagram and solve a more complex problem.*

Communicating About the Strategy

Don't forget to have students write and talk about their strategies. Impromptu teacher questioning and informal discussions help students solidify their understandings and provide opportunities for them to reflect on their approaches (see Figure 8–4). In addition, reviewing students' writing and listening to their discussions are great ways for teachers to get a glimpse into students' thinking. Try prompts like these:

- Why was drawing a picture a good strategy for solving this problem?

- Does a picture need to be detailed to help you solve a problem? Explain.

- Explain how your diagram helped you solve this problem.

- Can a picture or diagram help you find errors in your thinking? Explain.

- How did a picture help you better understand this problem?

Figure 8–4 *Ongoing teacher support helps students clarify their thinking and identify appropriate problem-solving strategies.*

CLASSROOM-TESTED TIP

Using Manipulatives to Introduce the Strategy

Many problems that can be simplified through pictures and diagrams sound quite confusing. Many students experience immediate anxiety and put their pencils down or their heads down, knowing that they cannot solve the complicated problem. The use of manipulatives is a great way to engage students in problem solving and show them that problems often appear more difficult than they may actually be. Begin by posing a problem like the following:

> **Pat folded his shirts and placed them in a stack. His yellow shirt was below his green shirt. His red shirt was above his green shirt. His blue shirt was between his green and yellow shirts. What was the order of his shirts from top to bottom?**

Provide each pair of students with a yellow, green, red, and blue cube and ask them to stack their cubes in the order that Pat stacked his shirts. Encourage students to talk it through with their partners as they create their stacks. Look around the room at the stacks of cubes to see which pairs may need help. Once students have the answer, talk about the level of difficulty of the problem. Was it easier than they thought it would be? What made it easier? What if they didn't have the blocks, how might they make it easier? The manipulatives allow students to do the problem one clue at a time, to simply move colors above, below, or in-between as needed, and is a way of recording or remembering what has been done. Once students' anxiety is lower, transition them into using paper and pencil sketches to do similar problems. Building skills and alleviating anxiety work hand-in-hand to create better problem solvers!

CLASSROOM-TESTED TIP

The Value of Modeling and Discussions

At times it becomes obvious that simplifying problems with pictures or diagrams may not be intuitive for all students. We notice that students become frustrated when we pose problems that appear confusing. It may be helpful to do some modeling for students, sharing our thinking, asking questions, and supporting them as we explore a problem together.

> There were 20 children at the Valentine party. Each child could choose the flavor of sherbet he or she wanted for a snack. $\frac{1}{2}$ of the children chose orange sherbet. $\frac{1}{5}$ of the remaining children chose lime. Then, $\frac{1}{4}$ of the remaining children chose raspberry. The rest of the children had lemon. How many children had each kind of sherbet?

While some students may immediately see how drawing a diagram is a way to simplify this problem, others will shut down as they are initially confused by the data. Support students by exploring the problem together. Ask them if seeing a picture of the problem might help them find the answer. Have them draw a picture to represent the 20 children, but rather than drawing children, ask them if there are other easier ways we might represent children. They might suggest circles or x's or slash marks. Ask students to select one way and draw 20 of them—one for each child at the party. Demonstrate for them on the chalkboard or overhead projector. Read the first part of the problem together and ask the students to circle $\frac{1}{2}$ to represent the children who ate orange sherbet. Label that section on your model "orange" and tell them that you don't want to forget what it represents. Ask them how many children still need to pick a flavor (10). Read the next part of the problem and ask them to circle $\frac{1}{5}$ of the ones that are left to find the number of children who had lime sherbet. Check to see if any students label the section lime and praise the idea so all can hear. Ask the students how many children still need to pick a flavor (8). Ask the students to circle $\frac{1}{4}$ of the remaining ones to see how many children chose raspberry. Have them label that section. Read the last part of the problem (the rest had lemon). Ask the students how many children had lemon based on what they see in their diagram. Have them circle and label the ones that represent lemon. Reread the problem. Ask the students how many children ate each kind of sherbet, this time having them use their drawing to help them. Ask students to talk about what was easy or hard about the problem and how the diagram helped them solve it.

Questions for Discussion

1. How can the use of pictures and diagrams simplify difficult tasks?

2. Pictures and diagrams help students visualize problems. How is the use of manipulatives similar to using pictures and diagrams? How is it different? How is acting out a problem situation similar to using pictures and diagrams? How is it different?

3. How might teachers help students see a variety of ways to picture or diagram a problem?

4. How might teachers challenge different levels of students in the same classroom?

CHAPTER 9

Strategy

Guess, Check, and Revise

> When problem solving becomes an integral part of classroom instruction
> and children experience success in solving problems, they gain confidence
> in doing mathematics and develop persevering and inquiring minds.
>
> —National Council of Teachers of Mathematics,
> *Curriculum and Evaluation Standards for School Mathematics*

The Guess, Check, and Revise strategy is exactly what it sounds like—if you're not sure where to begin, take a guess! The guess, however, should be reasonable and is only the beginning of the process. After plugging the guess into the problem situation, a student will need to adjust the guess until the correct answer is found. In the words of a third grader: "You guess and then you check. If it's too high, use lower numbers. If it's too low then use higher numbers." That sounds easy enough!

Beginning with a Guess

Often students are faced with a problem and they don't know how to begin. While a guess may be a good way to begin tackling the problem, the guess should be a reasonable one. Students should be able to use their number sense and estimation skills to get "in the ballpark." Discuss initial guesses with students. Together, look for clues in the problem that will help them make educated guesses and in so doing, lessen the number of revisions they will have to make. If a problem asks for three consecutive numbers that have a sum of 33, students should not be starting with a guess of 28. It would not be reasonable to think that 28, 29, and 30 would add up to 33. If you notice unreasonable student guesses, practice just the first step of this problem-solving strategy. Pose problems to your students and ask them to estimate (guess) the answer. Have students discuss the reasonableness of their guesses with a partner or team. Ask them to share their ideas on how they came up with their guesses. Logical reasoning and number sense play an important role in this strategy.

Revising the Guess

Revision is a critical step in this strategy. It is unlikely that students will guess the correct answer on the first try, so they must then plug their guesses into the problem and adjust the initial guess until they've found the correct answer. Students will need to recognize when their guess is too large or too small and will need to be able to make adjustments until the answer is found. Consider the problem:

> **Katie and Brendan played a game of Monopoly. When the game ended, Brendan had $50.00 more than Katie. Together they had $430.00. How much did each person have?**

Josh was confused and did not know where to begin, so he started with a guess.

> *"Katie had $200.00. So Brendan had $250.00 because he had $50.00 more than Katie."*

That would be a total of $450.00, which is too much. The guess was a reasonable one, but did not prove to be the correct answer. Josh needed to adjust his guess.

> *"Katie had $150.00 and Brendan had $200.00 so they had $350.00 together. That's not enough."*

Josh realized he needed to increase the amounts.

> *"$180.00 + $230.00 = $410.00"*
> *"$190.00 + $240.00 = $430.00. That's it!"*

Josh did several revisions before he arrived at the correct answer, but the revisions were thoughtful ones. He was using the data he observed to make each new adjustment. When evaluating student work, look for evidence that each revision leads students closer to the answer.

Thinking aloud is especially important when demonstrating this strategy. Both in selecting a first guess and in revising guesses throughout the process, it is important that students understand the thinking involved in each step. Students need to hear your thought processes as you adjust and readjust your answers. Students need to know it's okay not to get the answer on the first guess. After modeling a few problems for the class, you might want to ask students to work with a partner to hear each other's thinking during the revision stage.

As problems become more confusing, students may need encouragement to come up with their initial guess and may benefit from teachers setting up the problem with the whole class. Consider the problem:

Caroline's age this year is a multiple of 5. Next year, Caroline's age will be a multiple of 4. How old is Caroline now?

The problem initially feels complex, and students may not know where to begin. Teachers who acknowledge the confusing feel to a problem help to relieve initial anxiety.

TEACHER: This problem looks really confusing. Let's talk about it together for a minute. What can we do to make it simpler? Talk to your partner about a way to get started.

Students talk in pairs about ways to begin the problem.

TEACHER: What could we try?
STUDENT: We could just guess an age for Caroline.
STUDENT: We could try that she's 8 this year.
STUDENT: No she can't be 8, it's not a multiple of 5.
TEACHER: What do you mean?
STUDENT: The problem says her age is a multiple of 5 this year so we have to start with a multiple of 5.
TEACHER: So what might be a good guess? Turn to your partners and tell them a possible age for Caroline.

She asks students to share some of their possibilities which include 10, 25, 5, and 15.

STUDENT: We could say Caroline is 5 since that's the first multiple of 5. Next year she'll be six. But it won't work.
TEACHER: Why not?
STUDENT: Because next year her age has to be a multiple of 4 and 6 isn't a multiple of 4.
TEACHER: So this is getting confusing. Turn to your partner and see if you can come up with a way to make this less confusing.

Students share their ideas including one pair's suggestion that they could "make a list of all of the multiples of 5 and then add one to each one. Then we could find the one that is a multiple of 4."

TEACHER: Think about the different ideas that have been shared and work with your partners to solve this problem.

Whole-class discussions at the start of the problem give students a chance to process the task and think through a method of approaching the task. Now, they can use their knowledge of Guess, Check, and Revise thinking, their understanding of multiples, and their ability to organize and record data to gather the data they will need to find a solution (or more than one solution). Class discussions get students thinking about the task and focus them on some potential challenges and possible approaches.

Using Guess, Check, and Revise with Equations

A student might look at the following equation and not know where to begin. This is when students often put their heads down or choose not to proceed because they don't know how to get started. The Guess, Check, and Revise strategy will provide them with both a starting point and a method to figure out the answer.

$$\_\_\_\_\_ \times 2 + 10 = 26$$

Encourage them to try a number in the blank, for example, 4.

$4 \times 2 + 10 = 26$??? Actually, $4 \times 2 + 10 = 18$. "This answer is too small, so let's try a larger number. How about 6?"

$6 \times 2 + 10 = 22$. "Closer, but still too small. How about 8?"

$8 \times 2 + 10 = 26$. "It worked! 8 is the correct answer."

Without knowing how to begin, the student was able to find the correct answer by using the Guess, Check, and Revise method. While other students may find the answer in other ways (e.g., using inverse operations), our goal is to arm students with varied ways to find solutions and enhance their repertoire of strategies so they have options as they attempt the varied problems they face. Ultimately, our goal is for students to solve problems in the most efficient way possible, but the ability to guess, check, and revise to find an answer will offer a starting point for students who might otherwise be overwhelmed with the task.

Understanding the Role of Positive Attitudes

This strategy depends on the development of positive problem-solving attitudes as discussed in the Introduction. Students must be risk takers and be willing to jump in, even when they are unsure how to begin. Students are sometimes hesitant to guess an answer. Assure them that it is a fine way to begin a problem—as long as they check their guess and adjust it as needed. Students must also be patient and persistent as they check and revise each guess. Each guess should bring them closer to the correct answer.

Using Combined Strategies

While we are focusing on specific problem-solving strategies in this book in order to develop our understanding of each strategy, many problems require students to use the thinking skills from several strategies. Consider the following dartboard problem:

Sara and Chen are playing a game of darts. Hitting the center circle (the bull's-eye) is worth 15 points, the next circle is worth 12 points, the next is worth 10 points, and the outer circle is worth 8 points. How might Chen have scored 40 points in 4 throws?

Using guess, check, and revise thinking will lead students to reasonable possibilities, but students might also want to employ their skill of organized, systematic thinking and begin with the bull's-eye, try possibilities that make sense, and then move in a systematic way through the other data in the problem. While they are using organized thinking, they may only be trying those combinations that have the potential to solve the problem—their guess and check thinking may have already alerted them to combinations that could not possibly work as the answer (i.e., There is no reason to try 3 darts or 4 darts in the bull's-eye. It would just be too high of a score!). Combining their knowledge of guess and check thinking, their understanding of organized lists, and their knowledge of basic operations will support them in finding the solutions.

Building the Foundation for More Advanced Skills

Problems that are solved in middle school and high school with algebraic equations can often be solved by intermediate students using the Guess, Check, and Revise strategy. Consider the following problem, for example:

Lisa opened her book and saw the two consecutive page numbers. The sum of the page numbers is 43. What are the numbers?

In algebra, you write an equation: $x + (x + 1) = 43$. This equation represents an understanding that the solution can be found by adding a number (x) and the next consecutive number ($x + 1$).

In Guess, Check, and Revise, you try a page number, say 20. The next page would then be 21 (20 + 1 as it is the next consecutive number). The sum would be 41. That's too low. Time to revise! Try page numbers 21 and 22. The sum would be 43. The Guess, Check, and Revise strategy is another way to solve the same problem. Through sharing problem-solving approaches in the classroom, we begin to discover opportunities to transition students to alternate ways of representing problems. As students share their ideas, we might begin to discuss algebraic ways to find solutions, transitioning students to new approaches.

A Look at Student Work

Guess-and-check thinking is evident in the student work in Figure 9–1. The student recognized that cereal would not be a possible choice as it costs more than Manuel spent on both of the items that he bought. The student's first guess is close to the an-

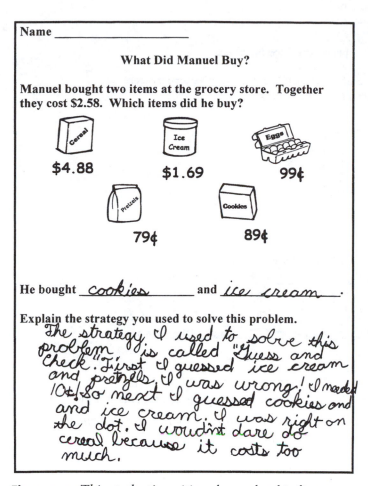

Name _____

What Did Manuel Buy?

Manuel bought two items at the grocery store. Together they cost $2.58. Which items did he buy?

Cereal $4.88   Ice Cream $1.69   Eggs 99¢

Pretzels 79¢   Cookies 89¢

He bought _cookies_ and _ice cream_.

Explain the strategy you used to solve this problem.

The strategy I used to solve this problem is called "Guess and Check." First I guessed ice cream and pretzels. I was wrong! I made 10¢. So next I guessed cookies and ice cream. I was right on the dot. I wouldn't dare do cereal because it costs too much.

Figure 9–1 *This student's writing shows that his first guess was a thoughtful one as he eliminated cereal as a possible item before beginning his search for the solution.*

swer, and his number sense and guess-and-check thinking allow him to revise his guess to quickly find the correct solution.

This kind of thinking provides a starting point for getting to solutions. The student writing in Figure 9–2 indicates that the student "didn't know where to start" and so employed guess and check thinking. Once the first guess was recorded, the student was successfully able to use revision to arrive at the correct answer.

Now consider the student work in Figure 9–3. In analyzing this student's work, it is clear that the student did not use thoughtful revisions, but rather just continued to try different combinations of numbers without considering what had been learned from her previous attempts. While she was moving through the data in an ordered way, she was not thinking about the sums. She accurately described her method when she wrote "I guessed and found the answer." She was persistent and did eventually find the answer, but she could have found the answer more efficiently had she thought about her guess and made reasonable revisions! *Tip:* Asking students to number their trials will help you assess whether their revisions are thoughtful ones as it will allow you to track the order of their trials.

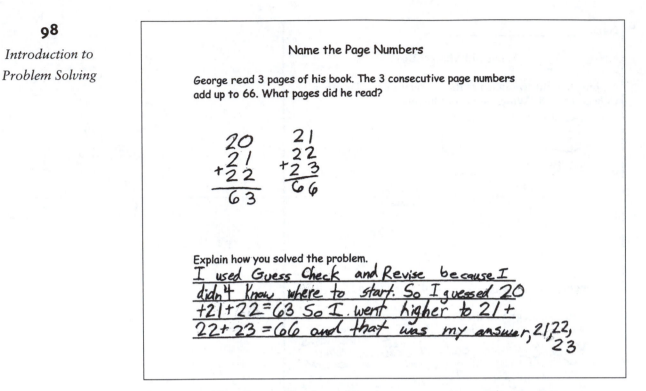

Figure 9–2 *The Guess, Check, and Revise strategy gives students a way to get started and then helps them use that initial information to work their way to the answer.*

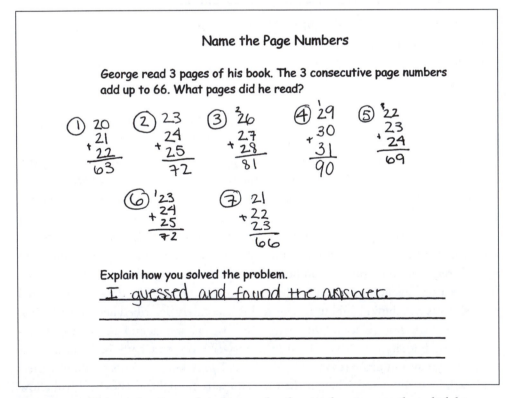

Figure 9–3 *This student's work indicates that her trials were not thoughtful ones.*

Communicating About the Strategy

In order to continue to develop students' understanding, don't forget to have students write about and talk about the strategy. Try prompts like these:

■ How did you come up with your first guess?

■ Explain why revising is so important.

■ How did Guess, Check, and Revise help you solve this problem?

■ Why did you choose this strategy to help you solve this problem?

■ Why is it important to be persistent when solving problems?

CLASSROOM-TESTED TIP

Modeling Guess, Check, and Revise Thinking

Cut out ads for five different items from a grocery store advertisement, for example, pretzels $1.25; cookies $2.50; chocolate cake $3.85; pizza $4.75; and watermelon $5.45 Tell the students that you bought two of the items and the total cost was $5.10 (or an amount that makes sense with your data). They will need to figure out which two items you bought. Have a student guess two items. Together, figure out the cost of those items. Ask the students to tell you if these two items cost too much, too little, or just the right amount. If the guess was not correct, tell the students that they will need to try again. Ask for another guess, but this time ask them to use what they now know to get closer to the answer. After the revised guess ask students, "Is the guess too high, too low, or just right?" Students may be asked to respond with thumbs up (too high), thumbs down (too low), or a flat hand parallel to the ground (just right). Ask students if there are any items that could not possibly be the items that you bought at the store and to justify why (i.e., watermelon because it costs more than the total cost or pizza because there is nothing you could add to it to get $5.10). Continue until you've found an answer. Try a few more, with students working in pairs or groups to allow them to discuss their guesses and revisions. Praise students for reasonable guesses and thoughtful revisions.

CLASSROOM-TESTED TIP

Cooperative Problem-Solving Cards

In order to stimulate group discussions about problem solving, consider dividing the problem data onto separate index cards and providing each group member with a card that states part of the problem data. Ask students to work together to combine their information and find a solution. For example, in a group of four students, each student might receive one of the following data cards:

Card #1   The class is on a field trip to the art museum. The cost for each adult is $7.00.

Card #2   The cost for each student is $3.00.

Card #3   The total cost of the trip was $91.00.

Card #4   If there were 25 people on the trip, how many of them were adults and how many were children?

Group members will need to share their information, consider everyone's data, and discuss their approach to solving the problem. A guess and check approach might lead them to the solution of 4 adults and 21 children, and the group discussions will allow members to share their confusions and successes. Refer to Cooperative Problem-Solving Cards on the CD for some examples.

Questions for Discussion

1. How does students' number sense impact their ability to effectively use the Guess, Check, and Revise strategy?

2. Can group and partner activities positively impact the development of the thinking processes needed to effectively use problem-solving strategies? How?

3. How might teachers emphasize the importance of reasonable guesses and reasonable revisions when working on Guess, Check, and Revise thinking?

4. How does the guess-and-check process in math compare with the trial and error process in science? Are there other connections between math problem solving and the scientific process?

CHAPTER 10

Strategy

Use Logical Reasoning

Reasoning is fundamental to the knowing and doing of mathematics.

—National Council of Teachers of Mathematics,
Curriculum and Evaluation Standards for School Mathematics

Logical reasoning is an important skill for solving problems. Many of the other strategies we have discussed depend on logical reasoning. Students may need to use logical reasoning as they create pictures or diagrams to represent confusing problem situations or as they employ Guess, Check, and Revise thinking to determine solutions to complex problems. In many cases, it is hard to separate logical reasoning from other strategies. Some problems, however, utilize logical reasoning as the primary problem-solving strategy. Whether it is the primary strategy or is combined with other problem-solving strategies, logical thinking is of critical importance to students' problem-solving success.

Logical reasoning is the process of thinking in an organized way in order to reach a conclusion. Logic problems often have lots of data that appear confusing and students are then challenged to make sense of the data and draw conclusions from it. The data does not always directly state ideas, but can require inferencing (i.e., *John does not use a bat to play his favorite sport. So, John's favorite sport is not baseball since that sport uses a bat.*). In this strategy, students need to practice analyzing clues or bits of information presented in the problem and then use that information to help solve the problem.

Techniques like process of elimination help students narrow down the possible solutions so they can arrive at a logical answer. Graphic organizers like matrices and Venn diagrams also help students organize data so they are able to clearly see the data and draw appropriate conclusions. Providing students with opportunities to experience varied logic problems and to discuss their conclusions helps them strengthen their logical reasoning skills.

The Role of Inferencing

When students are asked to inference, they are being asked to use clues to figure out what is happening in a problem. Often a problem does not come right out and state the necessary data, but rather challenges students to figure out the data by "reading between the lines." Consider the following problem that requires inferencing:

> Lindsay has a three-scoop ice cream cone. She has a scoop of chocolate, vanilla, and strawberry ice cream. The chocolate ice cream is the last flavor she will eat. The vanilla scoop is not touching the chocolate. What is the order of the ice cream flavors?

The problem is complicated by the fact that the data is not directly stated. Information must be gathered based on students' understanding of the situation and their ability to draw conclusions. If chocolate is the last flavor Lindsay will eat, then it must be the scoop closest to the cone. If the vanilla scoop does not touch the chocolate, then it must be on top. The order from top to bottom must be vanilla, strawberry, then chocolate.

Providing opportunities for students to share what is stated and what is inferred will help those who are confused by the problem. Class discussions, think-alouds in which teachers model their inferencing skills, and partner activities in which students can work together to discuss solutions are helpful instructional techniques. Inferencing is a critical foundation skill for effective logical reasoning.

Using a Logic Matrix

A matrix is a grid on which students record data. It is a tool for helping students organize information and keep track of their ideas as they work through the process of piecing clues together. Consider the following problem:

> Kathy, Lisa, and Dan each have a snack. One has a banana, one has a chocolate bar, and one has raisins. Dan does not like candy. Kathy peels her snack. Lisa's snack melts on a hot day. Which snack does each child have?

The information is confusing and somewhat jumbled together. In order to find a solution, students have to first find a way to clarify the data so they can look at it clearly to draw conclusions. Creating a grid or matrix like the one in Figure 10–1 allows them to organize the information. Students can begin the matrix by writing in the three names (Kathy, Lisa, and Dan) and the three possible snacks (banana, chocolate bar, and raisins). Then the clues are read, evaluated, and the conclusions recorded. The matrix supports students as they move toward a solution by allowing them to

	Banana	Chocolate bar	Raisins
Kathy	yes	x	x
Lisa	x	yes	x
Dan	x	x	yes

Figure 10–1 *Information is organized on a matrix.*

consider one clue at a time, and remember their conclusions since they have been recorded on the matrix.

> **Dan does not like candy.** (*Then he must not be having a chocolate bar—I can put an x by chocolate on the grid.*) Notice the inferencing!
>
> **Kathy peels her snack.** (*She must be having a banana. I can put a yes or check-mark by banana. That also means I can put an x by chocolate and raisins for Kathy, since she only had one snack. And I can put an x by banana for Lisa and Dan, since they must have had the other snacks.*) Eliminating wrong answers will help students narrow down the possibilities.
>
> **Lisa's snack melts on a hot day.** (*It must be chocolate! I can put an x by raisins for Lisa since I now know she had chocolate.*)
>
> *So, Dan must be having raisins for his snack!*

Each clue brings students closer to a solution. Inferencing helps students make sense of each clue, and the matrix helps them keep track of the clues.

When showing students how to use a matrix, remind them to read and think about each clue and to revisit clues a second time if the problem remains unsolved after once through each clue. Often, a clue has more meaning after another clue has been considered. Remind students that when they find an answer, they should eliminate the other boxes in the same row and column. There can only be one *yes* in each row and column. That is an important understanding, as a matrix is used when students are looking for a one-to-one match (e.g., which child ate which snack), so there will only be one child matched with each snack.

As students become proficient with using matrices, consider providing students with logic problems that do not have the matrix printed on the page. One of the challenges of problem solving is learning to select an appropriate tool for simplifying the process. Discussing familiar problems (ones solved in the past) and how they were solved often leads students to suggest the use of a matrix as a possible tool. And prompting students to create the matrix to solve the problem will advance their skills with this strategy.

Using a List to Organize Clues

A matrix is not the only way to sketch out a logic problem. Students can create lists on which they cross off items that are eliminated as possible answers. Figuring out what is not the answer can be an important step in finally determining an answer. Consider the following problem:

> **The Redskins and Eagles played a football game. The Redskins scored 34 points. Use the clues to figure out how many points the Eagles scored.**
>   **It is less than 38.**
>   **It is more than 27.**
>   **It is a multiple of 4.**
>   **The two digits add up to 10.**

Students can keep track of their progress toward a solution by making a list of numbers and then crossing off the unnecessary numbers as they analyze each clue.

It is less than 38, but more than 27. (*These are all possibilities.*)

28   29   30   31   32   33   34   35   36   37

It is a multiple of 4. (*That means it could be 28, 32, or 36, but I can cross off all of the others.*)

28   ✖   ✖   ✖   32   ✖   ✖   ✖   36   ✖

The two digits add up to 10. (*2 + 8 = 10. The answer must be 28! The Eagles scored 28 points!*)

 ㉘   ✖   ✖   ✖   ✖   ✖   ✖   ✖   ✖   ✖

 While some students may be able to do multiple steps in their heads without recording the data, many benefit from recording and eliminating data as they read and analyze the clues. And again, the process of recording the data ("get it out of their heads") can simplify an otherwise challenging problem. Hundred charts (see Hundred Charts on the CD) are another tool to allow students to "see" numbers when working with logic number problems. Students might use the hundred charts to record their ideas by crossing off or circling numbers to match the clues.

 In order to stimulate discussion about their thinking, consider having students work in groups of four to solve logic number problems. Give each student in the group a card with a different clue to the mystery number (see the logic examples in the Cooperative Problem-Solving Cards on the CD). Have students share their clues and work together to determine the mystery number. Consider assigning roles to each student (leader, recorder, checker, or reporter) to ensure that all students are engaged in the activity. And providing students with hundred charts to record their ideas will support them as number logic problems increase in complexity.

Using a Venn Diagram to Organize Ideas

Venn diagrams are also helpful tools in sorting out the clues in logic problems. Consider this problem:

> **The coach brought the 10 players on Brendan's basketball team to the ice cream parlor to celebrate their big win. The players could order an ice cream cone, a soft drink, or both. 7 players had ice cream and 6 players had a soft drink. How many players had both?**

Students can use a Venn diagram to organize the data for this problem. The Venn diagram provides a way for students to visualize an otherwise confusing problem. One side of the diagram can be labeled "ice cream cones" and the other side can be labeled "soft drinks." Each child can be given ten manipulatives (e.g., colored chips, pennies) to represent the ten basketball players. As students begin to represent the data on the Venn diagram, many will first place seven chips in the ice cream cone circle. As they try to place six chips in the soft drink section of the diagram, they find that they do not have enough chips. Students can be challenged to experiment with placing their chips on the diagram until they find a placement that fits the data in the problem. Working in pairs will provide students with opportunities to talk about the location and reason for their placement choices. As students see that they can slide some chips into the center of the Venn diagram, they are able to solve the problem (see Figure 10–2.)

Model your thoughts by speaking aloud as you solve logic problems with your students. Thinking is an abstract process, but through think-alouds and graphic organizers, you can help your students "see" logical thinking.

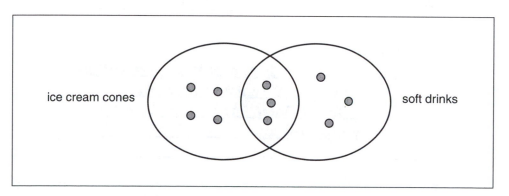

Figure 10–2 *Using a Venn diagram allows students to visualize the problem.*

A Look at Student Work

Students were asked to solve the following number logic problem:

> **Use the clues to figure out how many points the Roosevelt Raiders scored in their football game.**
>> It is less than 32.
>> It is a multiple of 6.
>> It is more than 15.
>> The sum of the two digits is 6.

While many students began by recording and eliminating information, recognizing that the data might be too much to do mentally, students were observed recording the data in a variety of ways. One student recorded all of the numbers from 1 to 31 and then began to cross off numbers. To explain his process he wrote "I wrote all of the numbers under 32. Then I crossed out the numbers that weren't multiples of 6. Then, I crossed out the numbers less than 15. After that, I crossed out the numbers that the digits didn't equal 6. I knew that their score was 24." His process was reasonable and led to the correct answer, but another student opted to record fewer numbers, writing the numbers between 15 and 32 on his paper and then following the clues to eliminate until the answer was found. The student work in Figure 10–3 shows a realization

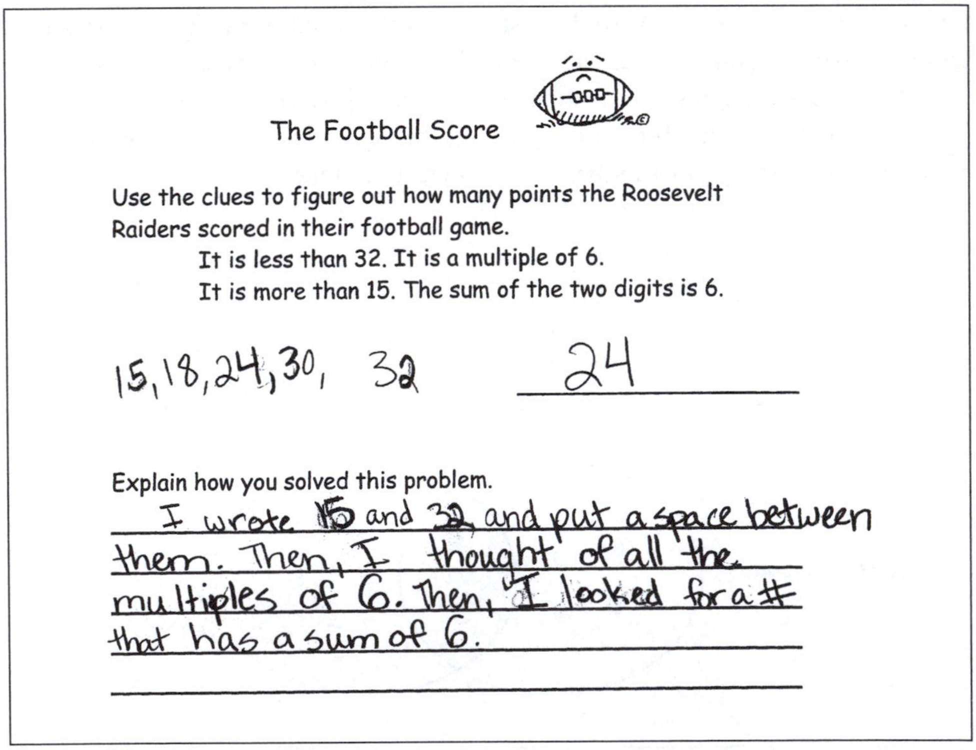

The Football Score

Use the clues to figure out how many points the Roosevelt Raiders scored in their football game.
> It is less than 32. It is a multiple of 6.
> It is more than 15. The sum of the two digits is 6.

15, 18, 24, 30, 32   24

Explain how you solved this problem.

I wrote 15 and 32 and put a space between them. Then, I thought of all the multiples of 6. Then, I looked for a # that has a sum of 6.

Figure 10–3 *Only multiples of 6 from 16 to 31 are recorded since this student took several clues into consideration before recording the numbers.*

that she only needed to record the multiples of 6 between 16 and 31. While each student got the correct answer, sharing their thinking will allow students to see ways to more efficiently arrive at an answer. In each case, the students used a list of numbers to help organize and remember the clues. As numbers were eliminated based on the clues, they were crossed off the list. And finding the number to match the final clue was easy as there were few choices left by that point in the process.

Students who experience problem-solving strategies in hands-on ways often use those experiences to make sense of similar problems when doing them independently. Consider the work in Figure 10–4. After using Venn diagrams in the classroom to visualize logic problems, the diagram became a helpful tool for this student, who was able to see the answer clearly after diagramming the problem.

The student whose work is shown in Figure 10–5 tackled a more complicated logic problem using a matrix. Her explanation indicates that the matrix made it easier for her to keep track of the clues and avoid getting mixed-up by the data.

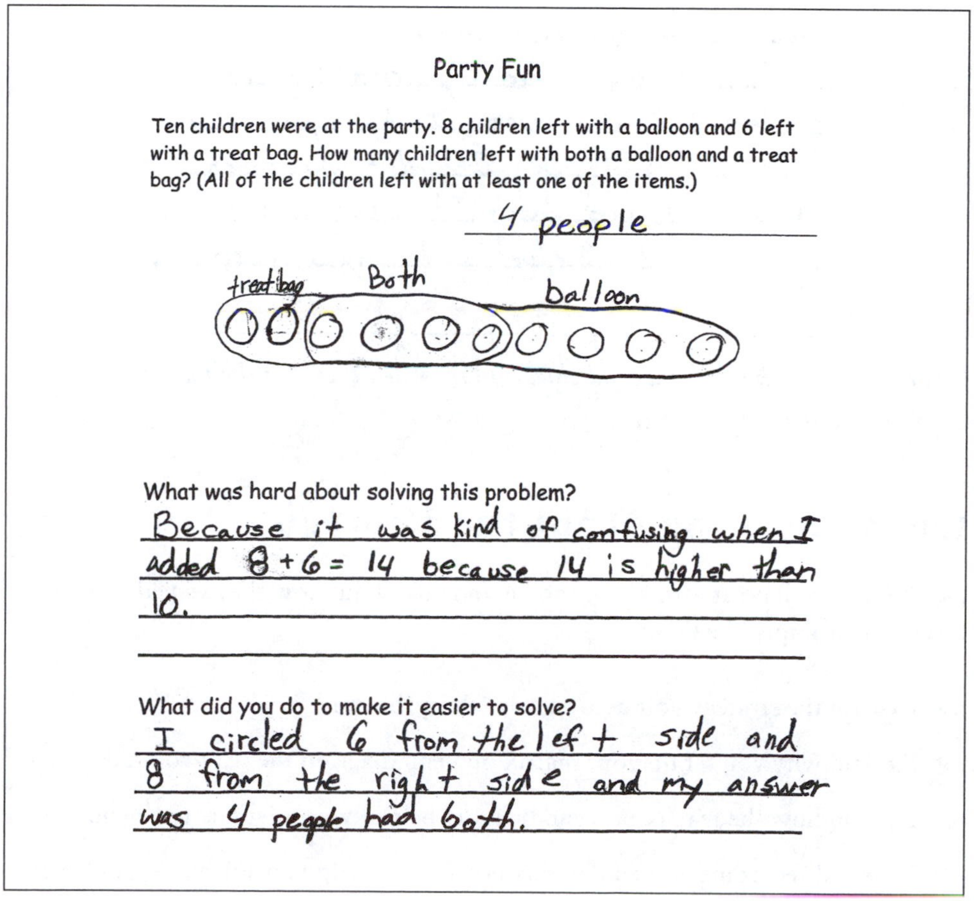

Party Fun

Ten children were at the party. 8 children left with a balloon and 6 left with a treat bag. How many children left with both a balloon and a treat bag? (All of the children left with at least one of the items.)

4 people

treat bag   Both   balloon

(O O | O O O O O | O O O)

What was hard about solving this problem?

Because it was kind of confusing when I added 8 + 6 = 14 because 14 is higher than 10.

What did you do to make it easier to solve?

I circled 6 from the left side and 8 from the right side and my answer was 4 people had both.

Figure 10–4 *This student used a Venn diagram to display problem data.*

The Pot Luck Dinner

Stacey, Kelly, Gail, and Joanie all brought their favorite food to the pot luck dinner. They brought cake, fruit salad, fried chicken, and potato salad. Use the clues to figure out which person brought which food.

	cake	fruit salad	fried chicken	potato salad
Stacey	✓	✗	✗	✗
Kelly	✗	✓	✗	✗
Gail	✗	✗	✗	✓
Joanie	✗	✗	✓	✗

- Kelly had to borrow a spoon to serve her food.
- Gail spent a while chopping ingredients as she prepared her food.
- Stacey was late because she had to let her food cool before she put icing on it.
- Kelly hates potatoes.

Which person brought which food?

Kelly - _fruit salad_   Gail - _Potato salad_

Stacey - _cake_   Joanie - _fried chicken_

How did using a matrix help you solve this problem?

It helped me by making it easier to make sure I don't get kids and food mixed up. It also was much easier to record data. It was easier to check the clues and my answer.

Figure 10–5 *As this student read clues and recorded them on the matrix, she began to see the data more clearly.*

Communicating About the Strategy

Don't forget to have students write about and talk about how they solved logic problems. Try prompts like these:

- Explain the strategy you used to solve this problem.

- Explain why you set up your matrix or Venn diagram the way you did.

- Explain how the matrix or Venn diagram helped you solve the problem.

- How did recording and eliminating possibilities help you solve the problem?

- What was difficult about this problem? How did you make it easier?

Introducing Logical Reasoning

To introduce the concept of logical reasoning to students, start with some hands-on activities. Ask students to manipulate objects based on a series of clues. One activity might be to give each student four shapes: a circle, a triangle, a rectangle, and a square (see Shape Template on the CD). Present the following clues and ask the students to put the shapes in a row from left to right on their desks based on the clues.

> **The first figure is a 3-sided figure.**
> **The figure with four equal sides is second.**
> **The circle is not last.**

Ask the students to share the order of their shapes with a partner. Ask them to discuss any differences and decide which order fits the clues. Walk around the room to visually monitor their progress. Have one pair of students explain why they placed the shapes in the order that they did. Point out to students that some information is stated while other information must be inferred, or figured out. If the circle is not last, where must it be? If the first figure is a three-sided figure, which figure is first? Remind students that using logical reasoning involves thinking about information and making some judgments based on what is known. Order the shapes in a different way, using different clues. You may even ask students to write their own clues and share them with their partner to see if their partner can order the shapes. Try similar activities, ordering different colors or familiar objects such as a pencil, crayon, eraser, and paper clip.

CLASSROOM-TESTED TIP

Hands-on Logic with Attribute Blocks

Attribute blocks are engaging manipulatives that stimulate students' logical reasoning skills. Attribute blocks are a set of blocks that come in five shapes (rectangle, circle, square, triangle, and hexagon), three colors (red, yellow, and blue), two thicknesses (thick and thin), and two sizes (large and small). Following are several quick and easy activities that use attribute blocks to strengthen logical reasoning skills:

1. Students might work in pairs or groups to find a mystery attribute block based on a series of clues.

    My block is green. (Blocks of any other color can be removed from the set.)

My block is not thin. (All thin blocks can now be removed. The mystery block must be thick.)

My block is large. (All small blocks can be removed.)

My block has 3 sides and 3 angles. (The large, thick, green, triangle is the mystery block!)

2. Attribute blocks can be used to explore similarities and differences using Venn diagrams. First, create a large Venn diagram for each group either drawn on poster board or created by overlapping two rings or hoops. Each circle is then labeled (place an index card beside it) with one attribute (e.g., *thin* by one circle, *hexagon* by the other circle). Students must sort the attribute blocks into the correct places on the Venn. All thin blocks will belong in one circle, all hexagons in the other, but all thin hexagons will have to be in the center section of the Venn. Blocks that are neither thin nor hexagons will be outside the Venn. Challenge students with triple Venns (3 overlapping circle) by labeling with 3 different attributes (e.g., thick, small, and circle).

3. Play a whole-class gatekeeper game by giving each student one attribute block from a set. The teacher is the gatekeeper and decides on one attribute (e.g., thick or yellow or square) that will allow the person holding it to enter through his (imaginary) gate. One-by-one students show their attribute blocks to the teacher and are either allowed to enter or asked to stand to the side (denied entrance). Students should hold their attribute block so all students can see it and the class must try to figure out the attribute that allows a person to enter through the gate.

Questions for Discussion

1. What is the importance of recording information when working on logical reasoning tasks?

2. How can teachers help students develop logic skills?

3. How does the use of lists, matrices, and Venn diagrams simplify logical reasoning tasks? How might students begin to recognize when each tool would be best used?

Strategy

Work Backward

Strategies are learned over time, are applied in particular contexts, and become more refined, elaborate, and flexible as they are used in increasingly complex problem situations.

—National Council of Teachers of Mathematics,
Principles and Standards for School Mathematics

Working Backward is reversing our thinking. We work backward to solve a problem when we know how a situation ends, but we don't know how it started. The strategy works well for problems such as the following: **If it's 2:00 P.M. and we just spent 15 minutes reviewing our homework, what time did we start reviewing homework?** or, **If I have $4.00 in my pocket after going to the grocery store, and I spent $2.50 at the store, how much money did I have in my pocket to start?** In each case, we are unsure what time or how much money we had to start, but can use the data in the problem to work backward to find the answer. In early grades we make it very concrete and simply ask students to "undo what was done" to get to an answer. By intermediate and middle grades, working backward can take the more abstract form of inverse operations. Simple one-step problems are a good way to introduce this strategy to students. Students learn to reverse their thinking—to begin with what they know about how the situation ended in order to figure out what happened at the start.

Working backward problems, as they increase in complexity, can frustrate intermediate-level students because of unknown data at the beginning of the problem. Consider the following problem:

Mrs. Higgins went to Burger Barn. She spent half of the money she had on lunch. Then, she spent $0.75 on dessert. She had $1.00 left. How much money did she have at the start?

Knowing that Mrs. Higgins spent half her money is not particulary helpful if we do not know how much money she had prior to spending half. Half is an arbitrary amount with half of 100 being different than half of 20 or half of 4. To effectively find this solution, students will need to begin at the end of problem with information that is exact ($1.00) and then reverse the actions to find out how the situation began:

> *"We know she had $1.00 left. The last thing she did was spend $0.75 on dessert, so let's say that she never spent that on dessert. Let's give her the $0.75 back. I'll add the $0.75 to the $1.00 she had and find that she had $1.75 before she bought dessert. Just before that she spent half of her money on lunch and was left with $1.75, she must have spent $1.75 on lunch because that would be the other half. $1.75 + $1.75 = $3.50. She must have had $3.50 at the start!"*

A critical step in ensuring student success with this strategy is reminding students to routinely check the answer. Because students often become confused when reversing operations, a simple check will allow them to find their mistakes.

> *"Let's see if that works. If Mrs. Higgins had $3.50 and spent half of it on lunch, she would have had $1.75 left. If she then spent $0.75 on dessert, she would have $1.00 left. That matches the data in the problem! I was right!"*

Recognizing Familiar Problems

To help students determine when to apply this strategy, it is important that we provide opportunities for students to talk through their thought processes as they are deciding whether this strategy might be appropriate. Past problems that were discussed with the class or explored in a hands-on way are often used as reference points in class discussions. Consider this problem:

> **Lucy had a bag of gumballs.**
> **She had 3 more yellow than red.**
> **She had the same number of red as blue.**
> **She had twice as many blue as green.**
> **She had 4 green gumballs.**
> **How many gumballs did Lucy have?**

While the problem may not initially look the same as the Burger Barn problem, there are similarities that should be discussed. It is these similarities, the familiar parts of the problem, which offer a clue to how it might be solved. The teacher questioning below guides students to reflect on the familiar parts of the problem.

TEACHER: What do we know at the start of this problem?
STUDENT: She had 3 more yellow than red.

TEACHER: So how many yellow did she have?

STUDENT: We don't know. It doesn't say.

TEACHER: What do you mean?

STUDENT: Well it just says 3 more but I don't know what that is. Like I don't know the number because I don't know 3 more than what.

TEACHER: So how could we find out? Does the problem give us any other information?

STUDENT: It tells us there are the same number of red as blue.

TEACHER: So does that help us? How many red are there?

STUDENT: I don't know. It's not telling us enough. We don't know the same unless we know how many there are.

TEACHER: You sound confused! Have we seen a problem like this before? Where we know some information but it is confusing and the only clear information we have is at the end?

STUDENT: It's like the burger problem!

TEACHER: How?

STUDENT: We didn't know what she had at the beginning. She had half. We had to look at the end.

TEACHER: So how did that help?

STUDENT: We just added what she gave away and got the answer. We could figure out half if we knew the other amounts.

TEACHER: What do you mean we added what she gave away?

STUDENT: We just did the opposite. If she gave it away, we gave it back to her, she subtracted so then we added.

TEACHER: So what do we know in this problem that might help us find the answer?

STUDENT: She had 4 green gumballs.

TEACHER: How will that help us?

STUDENT: Because we could use that and find out the others.

TEACHER: What do you mean?

STUDENT: Like we could know that she had 8 blue because she had twice as many as green.

TEACHER: So what are we doing to solve this?

STUDENT: We are starting at the end and going backward.

STUDENT: We are just reversing everything since we only know a number at the end.

The teacher's continued questioning guides the students to see the familiar problem. *Same*, *three more*, and *twice as many* caused the same problems as *half* had caused in the burger problem, but recognizing the familiar problem provided a plan for how to work through the confusion and get to a solution.

Increasing the Complexity of Problems

As students become proficient with simple work backward problems, we gradually increase the complexity of the task. This might be done by adding more complex numbers (e.g., larger numbers, fractions, decimals, percents) or by adding more criteria or changing the order of the information. Consider the following problem:

> **Caroline waited in line for the rides at the amusement park. She got on the log flume ride in $\frac{2}{3}$ the time that it took to wait in line for the roller coaster. The rapids ride wait was $\frac{3}{5}$ of the time it took to wait for the log flume. Caroline waited in line $\frac{3}{4}$ hour for the roller coaster. How long was the wait for each ride?**

This problem is a work backward problem with added complexity. Fractions alone can complicate a problem, and these fractions relate to time rather than just being fractions of whole numbers. In addition, the order of the clues provides a challenge for even those students who recognize that they should work backward because after determining that Caroline stood in line for 45 minutes for the roller coaster, they move up to the next clue (The rapids ride wait was $\frac{3}{5}$ of the time it took to wait for the log flume.) and find no information that helps them continue through to the solution. Instead, they now have to move up to the first clue in the problem (She got on the log flume ride in $\frac{2}{3}$ the time that it took to wait in line for the roller coaster.) to find information that will allow them to continue. The order of the clues has been mixed up to challenge students to locate the appropriate information. In this problem, students need to first recognize that working backward makes sense as a strategy, and then have to apply the strategy, use appropriate computations related to fractions and time, and simplify the problem by reordering the clues. Discussions about what makes a problem easy or hard, or how students can simplify confusing problems, are important components of problem-solving instruction.

Students might also be challenged with problems that require them to use their measurement skills with a work backward process. Rather than asking students to compute the perimeter of a garden, consider posing a problem in which students have to work backward to find the dimensions of one side of the garden as in the following problem:

> **Mr. Short had a rectangular garden. The perimeter of his garden was 48 feet. The length of his garden was 15 feet. What was the width of his garden?**

In order to solve the problem, students might begin with the knowledge that 48 feet is the perimeter, and then subtract twice the length of the garden (15 ft. + 15 ft.) to find out that the sum of the other sides was 18 feet. Since each side was equal in length, each side must be 9 feet long. By starting with the perimeter and working backward, students were able to find the missing data.

Working Backward with Equations

Another way to demonstrate working backward is to use simple equations.

$$\underline{\hspace{2cm}} + 3 - 1 = 12$$

Have students begin at the end of the equation. Ask them to think about what was done and work backward reversing the operations, to solve the problem.

"I have 12 now. The last thing I did was subtract one, so I'll add one. After that I can subtract 3, since I added 3 in the equation. What I have now should be the number I started with."

Remember, a very important step in the Work Backward strategy is checking the answer by plugging it back into the problem and seeing if it works. Remind students to always do this.

$10 + 3 - 1 = 12$. It works!

A Look at Student Work

When beginning this strategy with students, give them simpler problems to help them get a feel for the work backward process. As they become more confident with working backward, challenge them with problems that test their thinking with words like *half* or *twice as many*. In Figure 11–1, a student solves a problem that begins with half and is able to explain how she reversed her thinking to work backward to the answer.

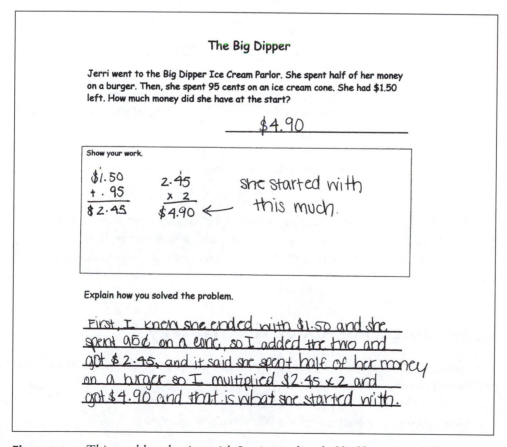

Figure 11–1 *This problem begins with Jerri spending half of her money. To determine how much she started with, the student must work backward to determine the value of "half."*

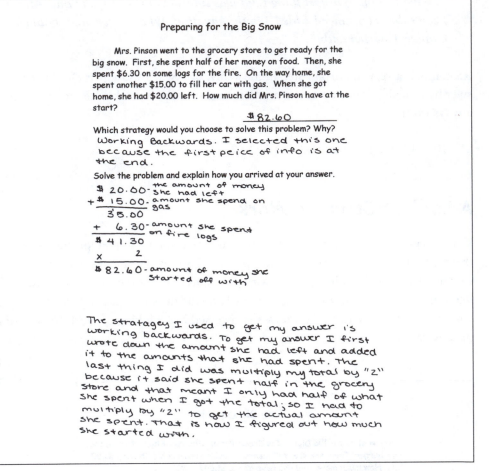

Preparing for the Big Snow

Mrs. Pinson went to the grocery store to get ready for the big snow. First, she spent half of her money on food. Then, she spent $6.30 on some logs for the fire. On the way home, she spent another $15.00 to fill her car with gas. When she got home, she had $20.00 left. How much did Mrs. Pinson have at the start?

$82.60

Which strategy would you choose to solve this problem? Why?
Working Backwards. I selected this one because the first peice of info is at the end.

Solve the problem and explain how you arrived at your answer.

$ 20.00 - the amount of money she had left
+ $ 15.00 - amount she spend on gas
35.00
+ 6.30 - amount she spent on fire logs
$ 41.30
x 2
$ 82.60 - amount of money she started off with

The stratagey I used to get my answer is working backwards. To get my answer I first wrote down the amount she had left and added it to the amounts that she had spent. The last thing I did was multiply my total by "2" because it said she spent half in the grocery store and that meant I only had half of what she spent when I got the total; so I had to multiply by "2" to get the actual amount she spent. That is how I figured out how much she started with.

Figure 11–2 *This student's writing reflects an understanding of the work backward strategy.*

Analyzing students' writing allows you to see if they have truly mastered the working backward process (see Figure 11–2). Asking students to both show their work and explain their thinking will help you better evaluate their understanding of the strategy.

Communicating About the Strategy

Remember to have students write and talk about the strategy they used to solve the problem. Try prompts like these:

■ How did working backward help you solve this problem?

■ Explain to a friend, who has never tried this strategy, how to work backward to solve a problem.

■ Why is working backward a good strategy for solving this problem?

- Why is it important to check your work after solving a problem using the Work Backward strategy?

- Write a problem that could be solved by working backward.

CLASSROOM-TESTED TIP

Introducing Working Backward

Give each student a small bag of candy (or plastic chips to represent candy) and a copy of the bag pattern shown in Money/Candy Bag Template on the CD. Tell the students that you are going to read them a problem. In this problem, they will know what happens at the end of the story, but they won't know how it started. Their job is to figure out how the story began. Just like a detective, they will be using clues to re-create what happened in the story. Pose the following problem to students:

> **Lisa had a bag of candy. She gave half of the candy to her sister. Then, she gave 3 pieces to her mother. She had 4 pieces of candy left. How many did she have to start?**

Ask the students to tell you how many pieces Lisa had in her bag at the end of the problem, after giving candy to her sister and mother (4). Have each student put 4 pieces of candy (or chips) in the candy bag (or by placing their chips on the bag cutout) to represent what she had at the end of the problem. Ask the students what happened right before Lisa was left with 4 pieces of candy. (She gave 3 pieces to her mother.) Ask them to imagine that she had not done that. Tell them that together you will be "undoing what she did." Each student should put 3 more pieces of candy into the bag, as if Lisa had not given them to her mother. Ask students how many pieces of candy are in the bag now (7). Then, ask the students what Lisa did right before she gave candy to her mother. (She gave half of her candy to her sister.) Ask students how many pieces half is. This may take some discussion or a visual demonstration on an overhead to show that whatever she had in the bag must be equal to the amount she gave because they are both half. Once students acknowledge that she must have given 7 pieces of candy to her sister, have them put 7 more pieces into the bag as if she had never given those pieces away. Ask the students how many pieces are in the bag now (14). Ask students if Lisa gave candy to anyone else (no). Have students count how many pieces of candy were in Lisa's bag to start (14).

Ask students to check their answer by acting out the problem with the 14 pieces of candy. As you read the story to the students, have them remove the candy from the bag as it is given away by Lisa. Do the students end with 4 pieces of candy just like Lisa? If so, their answer must be correct.

Try the activity several times, changing the quantities of candy given away. Exploring working backward in a hands-on way will help students visualize the work backward process.

CLASSROOM-TESTED TIP

Differentiating Instruction

Students within the same classroom often have varied experience and expertise with problem-solving strategies. It is important to present lessons that allow students to explore the strategy at different levels of complexity dependent on their needs. While all students might be involved in whole-class discussions about the working backward strategy, students can be grouped to allow some groups to explore more advanced tasks than others. Consider modifying problems for various groups to provide students with thought-provoking, but positive, experiences as they explore the strategy and refine their skills.

> *Beginning level*—Daniel bought a booklet of tickets for the carnival rides. He gave half of the tickets to Byron. Then he gave 4 tickets to Sharon. After that he had 6 tickets for himself. How many tickets were in the booklet that Daniel bought?
> *Developing level*—Daniel bought a booklet of tickets for the carnival rides. He gave half of the tickets to Byron. Then he gave half of what he had left to Sharon. After that he had 6 tickets for himself. How many tickets were in the booklet that Daniel bought?
> *Advanced level*—Daniel bought a booklet of tickets for the carnival rides. He gave $\frac{1}{4}$ of the tickets to Byron. Then he gave half of what he had left to Sharon. After that he had 6 tickets for himself. How many tickets were in the booklet that Daniel bought?

Posing problems at different levels will allow you to meet the needs of all learners within your classroom. The practice problems on the CD represent varying levels of complexity. Selecting problems, or modifying problems, to match the needs of your students will help them build their problem-solving skills. Other ideas for differentiating instruction for different levels of students include:

■ Have an additional component to the problem for groups that complete the first step (e.g., Tickets cost $0.50 each. How much did Daniel pay for the booklet of tickets?).

■ Vary the data in the second part of the problem to simplify or increase the complexity of the problem (i.e., Tickets cost $0.10 each—a simple computation, $0.35 each—a more difficult computation, or 2 for $0.45—involves some reasoning and computation).

■ Allow students access to hands-on materials to "act out" the problem.

■ Provide calculators to support students with the computations.

■ While some groups work effectively on their own, others may need your input and guidance, or even some modeling, to better understand the process.

Note: Cooperative group work is a great way to help all students refine their problem-solving skills. Both homogeneous and heterogeneous groups are valuable instructional formats. Heterogeneous groups (students of varied ability levels) provide an opportunity for students of different levels to learn from each other and hear each other's insights. But homogeneous groups allow you to select problems of different difficulty levels and allow faster-moving groups to extend their skills, and slower-moving groups to explore activities that challenge, but do not frustrate, them. Provide students with opportunities to work in both homogeneous and heterogeneous groups as they work on refining their problem-solving skills.

Questions for Discussion

1. Why do visual demonstrations or hand-on tasks help students better understand and remember strategies like working backward?

2. How might a teacher help students determine when working backward is a reasonable strategy to use to solve a problem?

3. How can an understanding of working backward support students when they are solving equations in algebra?

4. In what ways can teachers continue to challenge students as they develop their work backward skills? How might problems be made more complex?

12

Real-World Problem Solving

The excitement of learning and applying mathematics is generated when problems develop within the context of a situation familiar to students. Allowing them to formulate problems as they naturally arise within the context of everyday experiences gives them the opportunity to put mathematics to work, observing its usefulness and its applicability.

—Judith S. Zawojewski

The goal of problem-solving instruction is to have students build a repertoire of strategies with which they can solve real problems. Through practice with real-world tasks, they begin to develop their abilities to apply problem-solving strategies. In addition, they begin to see the value in learning the skills and processes needed to become successful problem solvers. The NCTM's *Curriculum and Evaluation Standards for School Mathematics* states, "Students need to see when and how mathematics can be used, rather than be promised that someday they will use it!" (1989, 35). Having students engage in problem-solving activities using real data from authentic materials, such as the newspaper, travel brochures, menus, or catalogs, will naturally show the connection between classroom skills and the application of those skills. Students will begin to see that problem solving occurs outside the math classroom, too.

Creating Meaningful Real-World Tasks

Although activities using real-world materials have been used in math classes for years, these activities have traditionally focused on functional (calculation) skills, as in the following menu problem:

Mary Elizabeth bought a hamburger for $1.25. She paid for it with a $5.00 bill. How much change did she receive?

In this problem, there is one correct answer: $3.75. The student is either right or wrong. In today's problem-solving classrooms, teachers are encouraged to develop problems that require students to employ more reasoning and thought when solving problems. This often means that problems become open-ended and individual students' answers may vary. An open-ended question using a restaurant menu might be:

You and a friend will be ordering lunch. You have $10.00 to spend. What will you and your friend order? How much change will you receive?

In this problem, students are still required to subtract to find their change. But, students now must work together to decide what they will order. Students first use their number sense and estimation skills to select some items to order. After adding their totals, they may need to adjust their decisions, as they may have overspent, or they may find that they have extra money and decide to add to their order. This problem provides practice with basic operations, but also stimulates thinking and encourages communication. Each student pair may have a different, but correct, answer. In the process of solving the problem, students will have practiced their reasoning, calculating, and communicating skills.

Problems involving a restaurant menu (see Figure 12–1) will also allow students to exercise and refine their reasoning skills by examining daily specials to determine if they are truly "deals." One local children's menu offered Kids' Meal Deals for $3.49. The Kids' Meal Deals included the regular meal, a drink, and a dessert. Students were asked to determine if this was truly a good buy. It is obvious from the student's response that not only did she practice many calculations in her attempt to find the

Figure 12–1 *Resturant menus provide real data for problem-solving experiences.*

solution but she employed her reasoning skills as well. The student first decided to calculate the cost for a variety of meal combinations when purchased separately, including the highest-priced meal with the highest-priced drink and dessert and the lowest-priced meal with the lowest-priced drink and dessert. After many calculations, she determined that even the lowest priced meal, drink, and desert were more expensive than the Kids' Meal Deal. In her own way, she justifies her solution as follows:

"Kids' Meal Deals is a better deal because it's less than the regular meal and a drink and a dessert. The highest with regular prices is $5.09. The lowest with regular prices is $3.69 and that's higher than the meal deal. You get the same food and it's less money."

She came up with a reasonable answer, and after discussions with classmates, she realized that she hadn't needed to calculate the cost of the higher-priced combinations in order to answer the question. The revelation that using just the lowest-priced items would yield the solution was the result of conversations with classmates and thoughtful review of the problem. When asked how she would change her strategy next time, she asserted that starting with the cheapest meal would be best because she might not have to do as much adding. (And she was right!)

Applying Classroom Skills to Meaningful Tasks

Investigations, which require students to incorporate thinking skills along with arithmetic skills, serve to challenge students. Consider the following task that challenges students to apply their skills in choosing the correct operation to a real-world situation. Fourth-grade students who had developed an understanding of key concepts for the operations through a series of classroom practice activities were asked to use their knowledge to determine the savings for purchasing festival tickets in advance. Students were given a brochure for a festival held each year in their local area (see Figure 12–2). They

---

Discount Ticket Offer

Buy Now and Save!

Regular Price	Advanced Purchase	Cost
Adult (16–61) $11.95	_____ Tickets at $10.00	_____
Senior (62+) . . . .$ 9.95	_____ Tickets at $ 9.00	_____
Child (7–15) . . . .$ 4.95	_____ Tickets at $ 4.00	_____
Under 7 . . . . .free		
	Total Cost	_____

Figure 12–2 *This brochure offers real data that allows students to practice their problem-solving skills.*

were asked to plan a family trip to the festival and calculate how much money they would save if they bought their tickets in advance.

Students first needed to calculate the cost of admission based on the advanced purchase ticket information on the brochure. In order to solve this first part of the task, students needed to multiply the number of adult tickets they were buying by the cost for each adult ticket, since each adult ticket cost the same amount (requires knowledge of the concept of multiplication). They also used multiplication to calculate the cost of senior and child tickets if more than one of either type was purchased. Then they had to add the cost of adult, senior, and child tickets to find their total cost, since each price was different (requires knowledge of the concept of addition).

After calculating the cost for their trip if tickets were purchased in advance, students had to recalculate the total cost using the regular admission prices, again using multiplication and addition when appropriate. In addition, they needed to use subtraction, since students were comparing the total cost of advance tickets to the total cost of tickets purchased at the door. This multistep activity asked students to use their knowledge of key concepts to solve a problem that required them to perform several operations prior to coming up with the solution.

Student writing is helpful in analyzing students' understanding of the final step in the problem—determining how much they would save if they purchased tickets in advance.

> *"I figured it out by subtracting the advance purchase price from the regular price and got $2.90. I subtracted because I compared numbers and that's when you subtract. I could see how much more one was than the other."*

Dependent on how many family members went to the festival and what their ages were, the students' savings differed. Each answer related specifically to each student's own data. In solving the problem for his or her family, each child was able to apply the math he or she knew to a real-world situation that related to him or her.

Similar problems can be developed from attraction brochures from amusement parks, zoos, museums, or water parks. Often, these attractions have special admission deals that are perfect for real-world problem solving. Consider attractions that offer individual admission rates and a family rate. You could ask students to determine if entering under the family rate would make sense for their family. Water parks and amusement parks often offer season passes. You could ask students to determine the number of visits they would need to make to the attraction in order to make the season pass the best buy, which would encourage reasoning while offering arithmetic practice. Family rates, special discounts, season passes, and consecutive-day savings all offer ideas for real-world problem-solving activities.

Utilizing the Messiness of Real-World Data

Unlike textbook word problems, real-world problems are not always clear-cut, easily defined, and composed of simple numbers. "Situations that allow students to experience problems with 'messy' numbers or too much or not enough information or that have multiple solutions, each with different consequences, will better prepare them to solve problems they are likely to encounter in their daily lives" (NCTM 1989, 76). When students use grocery ads to select items for a Thanksgiving meal, they may be faced with buying items that are sold by weight or in packages or sets (e.g., six soft drinks to a pack). This real-world data causes students to stop and consider how to proceed in solving the problem. Throughout the problem-solving situation, students must be aware of the data and make decisions based on how the data is presented in the real-world material.

> There are 10 dinner guests, but soft drinks are sold in multiples of 6—what should you do?

> You need 1 pound of turkey per person, but will you find a turkey that weighs exactly 10 pounds?

Students are faced with making sense of real data as they attempt to solve the problem, preparing them for future problem-solving experiences in a way that textbooks and worksheets are unable to do.

Discovering a World of Real Data

Real-world materials can be found everywhere. As you become aware of the role that real-world materials can play in your classroom, you will discover an abundance of materials that will motivate your students and provide meaningful, authentic mathematics explorations.

Newspapers

The daily newspaper is the most versatile real-world material because of its accessibility, affordability, and the variety of its data. Just one newspaper contains numerous examples of mathematics in action. Data is printed from the first page to the last, and you can use one issue for weeks without reusing a single article or piece of data. The currency of the newspaper allows teachers to capitalize on "what's hot" with articles about popular people such as politicians, rock stars, or sports heroes; current sporting activities such as the Olympics, or major league play-offs; or world events such as political elections or natural disasters. The newspaper is also very affordable. Many newspapers offer educator discounts that will enable you to purchase inexpensive classroom sets of newspapers for use with your students.

The variety of mathematics represented throughout its pages makes the newspaper an obvious reflection of the magnitude by which mathematics affects all parts of our lives. Each section of the newspaper contains unique information that reinforces a variety of skills. The daily weather section offers data about local weather and usually contains information about weather in other parts of the country and the world. The sports section provides game and player statistics and various tables that show team standings and statistics. You may find diagrams of sports fields, tables comparing player or team statistics, and graphs that illustrate sports data. Travel sections contain cost information for hotels or airfare to travel destinations. In addition, these sections frequently contain maps, complete with a map scale, to show the distances when traveling from one location to another. Amusement sections offer times and prices for a variety of entertainment events, and business sections provide a variety of graphs for your students to analyze. Classified advertisement sections include the cost information for placing ads, which allows students to calculate the cost of existing ads or write their own ads and determine the cost of running them in the newspaper. Newspapers often include food sections with recipes or home sections with home-improvement designs, including measurements. And all newspapers contain numerous advertisements. Ads for clothing, housewares, cars, jewelry, toys, or furniture can be found throughout the paper. Grocery ads also appear in the newspaper and provide data for a variety of activities including finding the best buys, estimating the cost of a grocery list, or planning refreshments for a party or family outing.

The variety of data appearing in the newspaper, combined with the material's affordability and accessibility, makes it a rich resource for classroom teachers. In addition, because it is a consumable (discardable) resource, teachers can create hands-on lessons that allow students to circle, cut, or paste newspaper articles or data. The ability to cut, mark, or paste transforms the newspaper into a hands-on tool, allowing students to be actively involved in a variety of math projects and investigations.

Restaurant Menus

Restaurant menus, particularly children's menus, which are available in many restaurants, are readily accessible real-world materials. The children's menus are often printed separately from the main menu and are sometimes given to children as placemats or coloring papers. They may be reproducible, with the restaurant's permission, and some restaurants are willing to donate a set to teachers on request. Carry-out menus also provide quick data for a multitude of math problems. Some ideas for math menu activities can be found in Real-World Problem-Solving Resources on the CD.

Recipes

You can select recipes from cookbooks or ask your students to bring in favorite recipes from home. Children's cookbooks often contain recipes with "kid appeal" that can be used to create highly motivating classroom activities. Recipe problem-solving activities require students to manipulate the data in the recipe in order to solve the problem. You could ask students to reduce or enlarge a recipe based on the number of people who will be served. They may be asked to formulate the grocery store list based on the ingredients needed to make the recipe. Ask students to use their reasoning skills to determine the fewest number of measuring cups and spoons that can be used while still being sure that measurements are exact. Some ideas for kid-friendly recipe books are also available on the CD.

Travel Brochures

Travel brochures are usually colorful, inviting, and filled with math data. Brochures from attractions that appeal to children will provide instant motivation for students to jump into an activity. Brochures from amusement parks, museums, historical sites related to social studies units, or local attractions that are popular with students contain high-interest data. Calculating admission costs for a family or a class, deciding on a schedule for visiting specific events when times are listed on the brochure, and calculating mileage to and from the location when a map with map scale is available are examples of some real-world math tasks that come to life with travel brochures. See Real-World Problem-Solving Resources on the CD for more ideas on travel brochure activities.

Travel brochures are available at the attractions themselves and are usually free of charge. Most attractions will be happy to give you multiple copies if they are available. Remember that students are encouraged to work together on problem-solving activities, so a brochure for each student is unnecessary. Depending on the task, teachers may only need a brochure for each group of two, three, or four students in the class. Brochures may also be obtained by writing to the individual attractions and requesting information. You can obtain addresses and phone numbers for local attractions by writing to, telephoning, or emailing individual state tourist board offices. Visitor centers on the interstates or hotel lobbies are great places to browse through brochures to find ones that are just right for your class.

Catalogs

Catalogs from sporting goods companies, clothing companies, and toy stores offer lots of interesting data for problem-solving activities. Because catalogs (unlike textbooks) are consumable, students can cut out pictures of the items they wish to purchase and include the pictures with their mathematical data. Students can create tables to show the items purchased, including prices and quantities. Ask students to select several pieces of clothing from a clothing catalog and make an organized list to show how many different outfits can be created. Students can construct tables to determine how much it would cost to buy one, two, three, four, or five of an item. Students may need to calculate shipping and handling charges which often requires knowledge of percents and are often dependent on the total cost of the order. Catalogs are generally free and companies may be willing to send you duplicate sets if they know you will be using them in the classroom. In addition, parents are often willing to donate outdated catalogs from home.

Grocery Ads

Most major grocery stores run specials each week. These specials are advertised in grocery ads that are inserted into newspapers or sent out through the mail. In addition, most stores have copies available for pickup as you enter the store. The ads are filled with price data and usually include pictures or graphics. There are lots of intriguing possibilities for math problems using data about food that is sold by weight, food that is sold in packs (e.g., six muffins in a pack), or food that is sold per item.

You might ask students to use the ads to plan menus for parties or family events. Ask them to select any item that costs less than $0.50 and then list all the possible coin combinations they might use to buy the item. Coupon shopping, combining clipped coupons and grocery ad prices, allows students to calculate the final cost of items that are purchased using coupons.

Students can be asked to bring in ads from home, or you can visit grocery stores on the last day of the advertised specials. Store managers are usually quite willing to give away the old ads when new ones are ready to take their place on the store shelves.

Sports Schedules

Local sports teams often publicize their schedules on free handouts. These schedules usually contain a series of calendars showing dates for home and away games, game times, and special promotion nights. Often, they also contain price information. The schedules can be used to plan imaginary outings to the sports events and calculate the cost of admissions. Calls to local teams should be all that is needed to get a copy of the current team schedule.

Sports Player Cards

Children have collected and traded baseball cards for years, and now football, basketball, and hockey cards are also available for trading and collecting. Each card is filled with data about a specific player. Students can compare players' performances, rank players based on statistics on their cards, or trade players to create a "dream team" based on the data on the cards. Logical reasoning games can be created using trading card data like the following in which students were given data from several players and asked to find the right player based on the clues:

I have a batting average that is better than (greater than) .300.
I hit an even number of home runs last year.
My number of hits is a multiple of 5.
Who am I?

Or, you could have students work with partners and write clues about the number of singles, triples, or home runs hit by their player. Following is an example:

He hit more than 20 home runs.
It is an even number.
It is a multiple of 6.
It is less than 25.
How many home runs did he hit?

The fun of actually being able to handle the cards, combined with the colorful photos on each card, makes the data more inviting than similar data that can be taken from a newspaper column. Player cards range in prices depending on whether they are the economy models or part of an exclusive series. For classroom activities, the inexpensive cards work well. Students can donate their old cards, or you can purchase inexpensive cards from local stores.

Nutritional Labels

Nutritional labels are on all types of food—the trick is to select foods that will appeal to students. Comparing the sugar or fat content in their favorite cookies may be more motivating than looking at the fat content of lima beans. Students could use tables to determine the grams of fat in 8 cookies, if the label indicates that there are 3 grams of fat in 2 cookies. Students might be given five food labels and be asked to use the Guess, Check, and Revise strategy to determine which three items they ate, knowing that they ate 14 total grams of fat.

Students can collect labels from home and bring them to school. You may want to have a box in your classroom in which students place the labels when they bring them from home. It may be helpful to have index cards available so students can glue the labels to the cards and write the name of the food product on the card. Cards can then be sorted by food category for storage until you plan to use them.

Advertisements

A variety of advertisements, often in a magazine format, are inserted in daily newspapers or received in households from mass mailings. Ads are available from a variety of stores including toy stores, department stores, drug stores, computer stores, or specialty shops. The ads usually list sale prices, sometimes calculated as half off or 20 percent off. Often the original prices are listed. Students can select gifts for their families or put together a birthday "wish list." You might select several items from one page in the catalog, calculate the total cost of purchasing the items, then give students the total cost of the items and have them use the Guess, Check, and Revise strategy to determine which items you bought from that page. Students could use advertised prices to determine reasonable exchanges. If they are returning an item that costs $21.95, have them decide which items they will get in exchange. Students can bring in ads from home or you might inquire at stores for multiple copies. And you may only need one copy with the class sharing the data.

Reaping the Benefit of Real-World Activities

Through open-ended investigations that require students to use real-world data, students will begin to view the mathematics they learn in class as a meaningful skill that connects to many areas of their lives. Along with giving students the opportunity to apply classroom skills, the open-ended problem-solving format offers students an opportunity to communicate about their mathematical thinking through group work and discussions. These investigations require students to use their reasoning skills to formulate plans and determine effective strategies for solving the investigations. Whether they are simple problems or more complex tasks, they direct students' attention to the everyday applications of mathematics.

Real-world materials are everywhere. The more you gather, the more you will discover. Stay focused on the NCTM Standards and the problem-solving strategies presented in this book to help you keep on track with your activities so that you develop not only fun activities, but activities that move students toward the math goals that you have set for them.

CLASSROOM-TESTED TIP

Problem-Solving Centers

Centers provide students with repeated practice in problem solving and are a great place to incorporate real data. Designing problems that use menus, travel brochures, or sports cards make engaging center tasks. Centers might simply pose a daily problem, with solutions available in an envelope at the center for student reference, or they might present problems for student pairs to discuss and solve. For a more exciting version, you might post a challenging Problem-of-the-Week (P.O.W.) each Monday, with students placing their solutions (and explanations) in an envelope at the center once they have solved the problem (see Figure 12–3). On Friday of each week, the teacher randomly selects one, or more, solutions from the envelope for review. A right answer and explanation earns the student a place on the POWerful Problem Solvers poster for the coming week!

Figure 12–3 *This student is hoping his solution and explanation to the center activity earn him a spot on the POWerful Problem Solvers poster!*

CLASSROOM-TESTED TIP

Math Mad-Libs

Connect problem solving to your students' lives and interests with some fun problem-solving mad-libs. Ask students to provide you with some words and numbers to insert into your math problems. You might ask a student to name *a person, a number from 1 to 10, a pet,* and a *cost between $2.50 and $5.00.* Then insert the student's responses in your mad-lib problem:

Example: _____ (person) was going to the pet shop to buy _____ (number) bags of food for his _____ (pet). Each bag costs _____ (money amount). How much did _____ (person) pay for pet food?

Do mad-libs as a whole-class activity asking different students to share a response to fill the blanks or allow students to work with partners to complete and solve their own mad lib. They will have so much fun filling in the blanks to create their own problems that they will be begging you to do mad-lib problem-solving again soon!

Questions for Discussion

1. In what ways would the use of real-world tasks enhance your problem-solving instruction?

2. What real-world data might motivate your students? What are some sources for real-world data that would be appropriate for your students?

3. What are the advantages of allowing students to use calculators when they work with real data? What are the disadvantages? How might you organize tasks to capitalize on the advantages and minimize the disadvantages?

CHAPTER 13

Assessing Problem Solving

Assessment should not merely be done to students; rather it should also be done for students, to guide and enhance their learning.

—National Council of Teachers of Mathematics,
Principles and Standards for School Mathematics

The Role of Ongoing Assessment

Teachers have traditionally viewed assessment as a culminating activity, providing information about whether each student has mastered a unit's content. Fortunately, we are beginning to recognize that assessment must take place throughout the instructional process. Ongoing assessment allows us to gather information about students' learning and monitor students' progress. It also helps us make sound instructional decisions by identifying those skills and concepts that need to be retaught or modified to ensure success for all students. Rather than being a final wrap-up of what was learned, assessment should guide our instruction to ensure that we are on track with our instructional activities. A thorough understanding of problem-solving assessment will guide you as you plan solid instructional activities that specifically address your assessment outcomes.

Because of the value of ongoing assessment in guiding the instructional process, it is critical that assessment and instruction be developed hand in hand. Consider our mathematics outcomes as our travel destination. Without a clear view of our students' destination, it will be difficult to determine the path they should travel to get there. But, with expected student outcomes in mind, instructional activities can be designed to move our students in the direction of their destination. Frequent assessment activities

Figure 13–1 *Listening to students explain their thinking is an invaluable way to assess their understanding.*

will ensure that our students stay on the right path and will help redirect those students who might become lost along the way.

During instruction, students explore and practice their skills under the guidance and direction of the teacher. Informal assessment should occur during instruction as teachers observe students at work, listen to their discussions, and question to check their understanding. During formal assessment, however, students are given opportunities to solve problems without teacher support. Problem solving may happen in groups or individually, but it happens without teacher guidance. These independent tasks provide an idea of how each student is progressing in his or her skill development. They provide information that will be essential for planning subsequent classroom lessons or valuable to share during individual student or parent conferences. Both informal and formal assessments allow us to analyze students' work for patterns in errors or clues to misunderstandings about the concepts we've taught.

In assessing problem solving, attention should be paid to both the process and the product. When analyzing students' problem-solving abilities, some very helpful types of assessment are teacher observations of the problem-solving process, interviews with students, and the evaluation of written, open-ended problem-solving tasks. Through analyzing both student behaviors and the products created during their problem-solving experiences, we can gather a wealth of information to assess our students' problem-solving abilities and plan for future instruction.

Finally, it is important to recognize that what we think we have taught is not always what students have learned. Despite our belief that a concept was fully explained or a process was sufficiently modeled, if students are still confused, it is our responsibility to think of new ways to address it until they have learned it. Ongoing assessment helps us determine when clarification, revision, or reteaching is appropriate.

The Value of Observations

Much information can be gained about students' understanding of the problem-solving process through classroom observations. As students solve problems in pairs or groups, the teacher should circulate throughout the classroom, assessing students' understanding of the process. By listening to group discussions, the teacher can gather valuable information regarding students' understanding of the problem, their ability to work together and share ideas as they work toward a solution, and their ability to judge the reasonableness of both their plan and, ultimately, their solution. As students explain their ideas to other group members or challenge others' thinking, we gather information about each student's level of expertise. These observations can be informal and used simply to get a general sense of class abilities, or they can be formal observations in which checklists are used to evaluate individual students or groups of students. Teacher-developed checklists help us gather information on students' ability to collaborate, reason, and problem solve. You will find a Problem-Solving Group Observation Checklist on the CD.

Observation checklists may also be designed for individual student assessment. Checklist items might include whether a specific student contributed to the problem-solving activity, was able to restate a problem or explain a solution, or contributed a reasonable strategy to the group's discussion. Whether observations are formal or informal, they provide insight into students' understanding of the problem-solving process. Post-observation conferences with individuals or groups allow us to discuss our observations with students and help them see the value of collaborative problem solving.

The Value of Interviews

Student interviews provide tremendous insight into students' problem-solving skills. In talking with individual students about a specific problem-solving task, the teacher gains an understanding of the student's thinking as he or she approached the task. Interviews allow us to ask questions like "Why did you decide to do that?", "Did you have any difficulties as you were trying to solve this problem?", or "Was there any other way you could have solved this?" Interviews provide us with the background information to understand what we see on a student's paper.

Interviews can be formal or informal. Some teachers like to set up formal conferences. As the class is working on a task, individual students are asked to meet with the teacher for a brief conference. With their papers in hand, students are asked to explain, justify, or describe their thinking. Informal conferences also provide valuable information. As students are working on problem-solving activities, the teacher might pull a chair up to a pair or an individual student and ask some probing questions to better understand their thinking. Whether formal or informal, interviewing students can shed light on their understanding of the problem-solving process.

The Value of Rubrics in Assessment

Written assessment tasks provide information on individual students' problem-solving abilities. While multiple-choice tests may be appropriate in some mathematical situations, open-ended assignments provide much more information when assessing problem solving. Students' responses to open-ended problem situations provide us with valuable information about their level of understanding of the problem-solving process.

To be most effective, scoring keys should be developed before instruction takes place. In this way, we can focus on what we want students to learn and then design instructional tasks that will get them there. A general scoring key that can be applied to a set of activities is called a *rubric*. The use of rubrics to assess problem-solving activities offers students a chance to see what is expected of them before they begin a problem-solving task. It can help guide them as they work through a problem, reminding them of the important points to consider in solving the problem. After their task is scored, it allows them to see the degree to which they were able to meet the assessment criteria, and therefore, it becomes a valuable tool in helping them understand how they can improve their work.

Rubrics can be *holistic* (assessing the students' ability to perform the task as a whole) or *analytic* (assessing the degree to which students demonstrate their proficiency on a specific outcome). The type of rubric we choose will depend on the assessment information we wish to gain.

A Holistic Rubric for Problem Solving

A holistic rubric rates the student's ability to complete a task that is a compilation of several outcomes. Problem solving is such a task. There are several key outcomes that we look for when assessing students' problem-solving skills.

First, students should be able to select and use an appropriate strategy. Not all students will select the same strategy, but each selection should make sense as a means to solve the problem (see Figure 13–2).

Second, students should be able to find a correct solution. There may be more than one correct solution. Students' solutions need to make sense with the data they have at hand. In addition, students' answers need to be the result of correct calculations.

Third, students need to be able to communicate about their problem solving. Our students' abilities to communicate their thoughts about solving problems provide us with a clearer picture of each student's level of knowledge. Their writing offers insight into the process they went through to arrive at their answer. It often provides information about which we might otherwise need to conjecture. In light of the strong em-

Student A

Cartons of Milk

1. The school cafeteria sells chocolate milk and white milk. If 2
cartons of white milk cost $0.90, how much will 8 cartons of
white milk cost?

$3.60

cartons	2	4	6	8
cost	90¢	$1.80	$2.70	($3.60)

Explain how you solved the problem.

1. I made a table showing the cartons and costs.
2. I wrote 90¢ under 2 cartons.
3. I kept adding 90¢ each time.
The answer is $3.60.

Student B

Cartons of Milk

1. The school cafeteria sells chocolate milk and white milk. If 2 cartons of
white milk cost $0.90, how much will 8 cartons of white milk cost?

$3.60

Show your work.

$0.90
× 4
$3.60

2 cartons = 90¢
2 × 4 = 8 cartons

Explain how you solved the problem.

I multiplied $0.90 × 4 and
got $3.60 and that was my
answer.

Figure 13–2 *These students used different, but both reasonable, strategies for
solving the problem.*

phasis of the NCTM Standards regarding the development of mathematical communication, it is recommended that writing be integrated into the problem-solving process and become a part of the holistic rubric.

Once teachers have set outcomes for their students, developing a problem-solving rubric becomes easy. As students look at their completed problems, they are able to see the outcomes they have met and those that they have not yet mastered. With this information in mind, they become able to revise their work to move closer to exemplary quality work.

Figure 13–3 is a holistic rubric for problem-solving activities. First, the rubric lists the expected student outcomes, then it outlines the criteria needed to earn scores ranging from 0–4.

Expected Student Outcomes:

Students will be able to

1. select and use an appropriate strategy.

2. calculate a correct answer.

3. explain their strategy for solving the problem.

Problem-Solving Rubric:

4 – arrived at a correct answer; used an appropriate strategy; adequately explained answer

3 – used an appropriate strategy; calculated a correct answer but was unable to explain the strategy; *or* adequately explained the strategy but did not calculate a correct answer

2 – used an appropriate strategy; did not find a correct answer; could not explain the strategy

1 – attempted to solve the problem, but completely incorrect in attempt

0 – no attempt/blank

Figure 13–3 *Rubrics are designed with expected student outcomes in mind.*

This rubric offers a quick and easy way to assess our students' ability to solve problems. In this rubric, the selection of an appropriate strategy, the calculation of a correct answer, and the effective written explanation of the answer are the expected student outcomes. The ultimate goal is that students are able to meet all three outcomes as a demonstration of their problem-solving skills. Students who have seen the rubric prior to the activity will be focused on these three important outcomes that they are expected to demonstrate. In this way, the rubric helps guide students through the problem-solving experience.

In order to score a 2 or higher, students must demonstrate their ability to select and use an appropriate strategy. Selecting a reasonable strategy is the foundation for good problem solving. If a student lacks the ability to think through a situation and decide on a plan for solving the problem, his or her correct answer may be no more than a lucky guess. Students who are also able to find a correct answer based on an appropriate strategy and explain the strategy they selected will receive higher scores to correlate with their greater ability to complete the problem-solving task.

While the first two expected outcomes (selecting an appropriate strategy and calculating a correct answer) will always remain the same, the final outcome may be reworded to direct students to different types of mathematical communication. Some examples might include justifying the solution or explaining why a particular strategy was used. In each case, the outcome of strengthening mathematical communication is addressed with a slightly different writing assignment.

The Role of Rubrics in Improvement

The rubric is an effective tool for guiding students in revising their problem solving. Many teachers allow students to rewrite responses after the initial scoring. This technique encourages students to focus on the rubric and attempt to improve their writing and increase their score. Much like a revision checklist helps students polish a written composition in language arts class, the rubric guides students in their mathematical revision process.

Evaluating My Problem Solving, which is found on the CD, will direct students through an analysis of their work. As students review their own work with the rubric in mind, they are able to see ways in which they can improve. The ability of students to analyze and improve their own work is our ultimate goal, as it indicates that students have internalized the strategies we have taught.

Analytic Rubrics for Assessing Specific Skills

While with the holistic rubric, the goal is to have students demonstrate their ability to perform all three outcomes in order to successfully complete the task, the analytic rubric looks in more detail at the degree to which one outcome has been mastered. Analytic rubrics assess the degree of correctness or completeness of students' calculations or responses. With this type of rubric, each of our problem-solving outcomes—students' ability to select and use an appropriate strategy, students' ability to calculate a correct answer, and students' ability to explain their thinking—can be judged individually as to the degree to which the student has mastered it. This type of rubric is valuable in that it allows us to identify specific strengths and weaknesses. We are then able to address weaknesses with additional instruction.

Outcome 1: Select and Use an Appropriate Strategy

An important problem-solving skill is the ability to identify and use an appropriate strategy. It is not necessary that the student select the same strategy that we had in mind when designing the problem. Remember the different strategies selected by the students in Figure 13–2. For each problem, we must look at a student's work and determine the reasonableness of the strategy that he or she selected. The degree to which the student can carry out the selected strategy can be assessed with the analytic rubric in Figure 13–4.

Outcome 2: Calculate a Correct Answer

Calculating the correct answer is an important part of the problem-solving process. Often, calculations require several operations and students can make small errors, despite showing evidence that they understand the arithmetic operations that would lead to a correct answer. At other times, students appear to be confused from the start and make multiple errors in calculating an answer. By using the rubric shown in Figure

---

Expected Student Outcome:

Students will be able to select and use an appropriate problem-solving strategy.

Rubric for Selecting an Appropriate Strategy:

4 – reasonable strategy selected and fully developed, including diagrams or labeled work to support the strategy

3 – reasonable strategy selected; moderately developed

2 – reasonable strategy selected, but minimally developed; major errors may be evident

1 – strategy choice is inappropriate for problem

0 – no attempt/blank

Figure 13–4 *This rubric assesses a student's ability to select an appropriate problem-solving strategy.*

13–5 when assessing a student's ability to correctly calculate an answer, we are able to gather valuable information about the student's skills. *Note:* There are some problem-solving strategies for which this rubric would not be applicable. For example, if students are drawing a picture or diagram to solve a problem, no calculations may be necessary. The rubric may also be unnecessary for simple one-step computations.

Expected Student Outcome:

Students will be able to correctly calculate the answer to the problem.

Calculation Rubric:

4 – calculations are completely correct and answers are properly labeled

3 – calculations are mostly correct; minor errors may occur

2 – calculations contain major errors

1 – calculations are completely incorrect

0 – no attempt/blank

Figure 13–5 *This rubric assesses a student's ability to correctly calculate an answer.*

Outcome 3: Communicate Mathematically

When teaching students how to explain their work or justify their solutions in writing, using a rubric that addresses only the explanation part of the answer will help them focus on and improve their communication skills. Developing good writing skills requires practice. A rubric like the one in Figure 13–6 will help students see the components of a well-written response.

The responses to the following problem illustrate the varying degrees to which students might demonstrate their ability to communicate mathematically.

SAMPLE PROBLEM:
For the school cupcake sale, parents made chocolate, yellow, and lemon cup-cakes. They iced them with chocolate, vanilla, and swirl icing. How many different cake and icing combinations are possible?

Question: How can you be sure you listed every possible combination?

Score—4

"I got my answer by listing out my choices. First I wrote down the first kind of cake and wrote all the icing choices with it. Then I crossed out chocolate cake and went to yellow cake and did the same thing. Then I crossed out yellow in the problem and went to lemon. I continued until I crossed out all the cake choices. I had chocolate with chocolate, chocolate with vanilla, and chocolate with swirl. Then I had yellow with chocolate, yellow with vanilla, and yellow with swirl. Then I had lemon with chocolate, lemon with vanilla, and lemon with swirl. I did them in order so I wouldn't miss any."

This student clearly explained how he made a list using each type of cupcake and each type of icing. He gave examples to support his thinking. He mentioned the importance of making his list in an organized way and indicated that he crossed off items after he exhausted them on his list. This student's thinking was clearly conveyed.

Expected Student Outcome:

Students will be able to clearly explain the strategy they used to solve the problem.

Mathematical Communication Rubric:

4 – exemplary explanation; detailed and clear; may have provided examples

3 – explanation contained adequate details; adequate clarity

2 – explanation somewhat clear; lacks details

1 – attempted an explanation, but incorrect or unclear

0 – no attempt/blank

Figure 13–6 *This rubric assesses a student's ability to communicate mathematical ideas.*

Score–3

*"I listed each kind of icing under each kind of cupcake, so I can be sure I got all of
the combinations."*

This student understood that the goal was to list each type of cupcake and then
each kind of icing until all possibilities were used. The explanation is brief but correct
and adequate.

Score–2

"I put all the cupcakes and icings together."

This student's response lacks clarity. He mentions "all" the cupcakes and icings, so
he may have the idea, but it is unclear whether the student used the strategy correctly.
This student needs to explain in more detail.

Score–1

*"I know I listed possible combinations because I have seen and tasted these combi-
nations that I listed."*

This student's response addresses, but does not answer, the question about possible combinations. An attempt was made.

Score–0
blank

This student did not attempt to answer the question.

You can assist students in strengthening their problem-solving abilities and developing their writing skills in several ways. Think-alouds that model well-developed
explanations provide students with examples of logical thinking. And discussions
among partners or groups, during which students can share their ideas, help students
develop a variety of ways to explain their thinking process.

Problem solving is a thinking skill. In order to monitor how students' thinking
is progressing, it is important to frequently ask students to share their thoughts both
orally and in writing. Students' writing allows us to recognize difficulties or misunderstandings they might be experiencing. It offers a valuable glimpse into their thinking processes and allows us to determine if they are progressing smoothly in their
understanding of the problem-solving process.

A major benefit of frequent assessment of student work is the insight it provides
for modifying our instruction. In Figure 13–7, the student moved in a systematic way
through the data, but rather than recording the data in a separate list, she drew lines
to show the combinations tried. In doing so, she noticed that each of the 4 cookies were
matched with 3 drinks and recognized that 3×4 would work to solve the problem.
While the drawing of lines worked for that student (and with this limited data), the
student in Figure 13–8 began in the same way but then had trouble deciphering the
lines he had drawn and ended up with a wrong answer. An analysis of their work provides insights into how to better support them. Having recognized the need for moving in a systematic way and recording their ideas, the students would now benefit
from diagramming the data in a way in which the lines would not blur together. An-

> **Special Cookie Deals**
>
> Rita's Cookie Shop is selling cookie combos (one cookie and one drink) for a special price. She created this poster to advertise her combos, but needs help completing the final line.
>
> | Rita's Cookie Shop |
> | --- |
> | Try a cookie combo for just $1.50! |
> | Choose one cookie and one drink. |
>
> | Cookies | Drinks |
> | --- | --- |
> | chocolate chip | milk |
> | oatmeal | lemonade |
> | sugar | fruit punch |
> | peanut butter | |
>
> Try all _12_ of our tasty combos!
>
> How many possible cookie and drink combinations are sold at Rita's Cookie Shop? Show your work and explain how you know you figured out all of them.

Chocolate chip — milk
Oatmeal — lemonade
Sugar — fruit punch
peanut butter

I started with chocolate chip and I connected it to all three drinks. Then I did oatmeal and connected it to all three drinks. Next I did the sugar and connected it to all three drinks. Finally I used peanut butter and connected it to all three drinks. After that I did 3×4=12 combinations.

Figure 13–7 *This student demonstrated an understanding of organized thinking, but as problems increase in complexity her technique of drawing lines may get confusing.*

alyzing their work indicates that discussions about tree diagrams may be the perfect next step.

Self-Reflections on Problem Solving

Teachers should offer students opportunities to reflect on their problem solving through journal writing, allowing them to express their successes and frustrations as they develop as problem solvers. Problem-solving journals that allow students to reflect on daily or weekly lessons provide us with insight into our students' perceptions, confusions, and successes. See Relecting on Problem Solving on the CD for ideas for open-ended journal writing prompts. Journal writing should not be scored, although teacher comments are recommended. Teacher/student dialogues can begin through

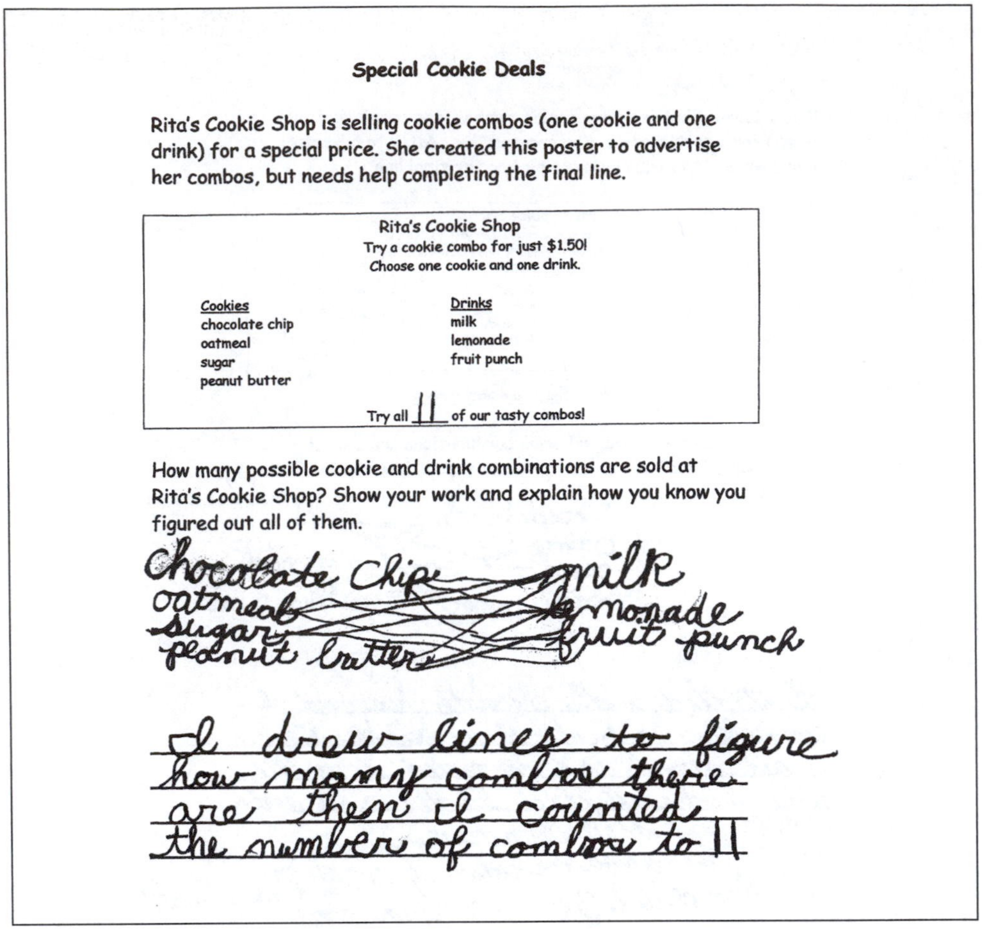

Special Cookie Deals

Rita's Cookie Shop is selling cookie combos (one cookie and one drink) for a special price. She created this poster to advertise her combos, but needs help completing the final line.

Rita's Cookie Shop
Try a cookie combo for just $1.50!
Choose one cookie and one drink.

Cookies
chocolate chip
oatmeal
sugar
peanut butter

Drinks
milk
lemonade
fruit punch

Try all ___ of our tasty combos!

How many possible cookie and drink combinations are sold at Rita's Cookie Shop? Show your work and explain how you know you figured out all of them.

Chocolate Chip   milk
oatmeal   lemonade
sugar   fruit punch
peanut butter

I drew lines to figure
how many combos there
are then I counted
the number of combos to 11

Figure 13–8 *While this student may have the appropriate thinking skills, his diagram led to an incorrect answer.*

journal writing in which we encourage our students and point out their growth and successes.

Varied Assessment

Both holistic and analytic rubrics are valuable ways to analyze students' progress. Whether we are assessing students' ability to put together the needed skills to effectively solve problems (holistic rubrics) or analyzing strengths and weaknesses in a specific outcome area (analytic rubrics), a great deal of information can be gained from frequent assessment. Teacher observations, student interviews, and student self-reflections also contribute important data to the assessment process. Ongoing and varied assessment throughout the teaching process will provide the information we need to make strong instructional decisions and, ultimately, create a classroom filled with successful problem solvers.

Using Rubrics to Improve Mathematical Communication Skills

One way to help students see the degree to which an explanation is clear and detailed is to evaluate writing samples as a class. Write several responses of your own, with varying degrees of clarity, and have students score them using the rubric. Students can use an all-pupil response method such as raising the number of fingers to show the score they would give each writing sample. As students give a score to the writing sample, have them justify the score using the criteria in the scoring key. Together, the class can rewrite the sample to give it a higher score.

Another technique that helps students learn to use a rubric to guide revision is compiling a list of responses with scores of 1, 2, 3, and 4. In pairs or groups, the students discuss and evaluate the differences between the writing samples and attempt to determine what is missing in the responses that scored 1, 2, and 3. Together, each group works to rewrite the 1 to make it a 2 or better, the 2 to make it a 3 or better, or the 3 to make it a 4. Groups can then present their revised writing to the class.

Showing students concrete examples of how to improve their writing with details, examples, and clarity of thought will help them strengthen their skills in communicating about their math thinking.

Questions for Discussion

1. Why is problem solving frequently scored using a rubric rather than simply by the correct answer?

2. What can teachers learn through students' communication about their problem solving?

3. What does it mean to say that we assess both product and process during problem solving instruction?

14

Problem Solving Across
the Content Standards

The kinds of experiences teachers provide clearly play a major role in determining the extent and quality of students' learning.

—National Council of Teachers of Mathematics,
Principles and Standards for School Mathematics

We have been focusing on the importance of helping students develop the process skill of problem solving to allow them to effectively explore math ideas and generate solutions. We have seen that problem solving, while a critical process skill, does not stand alone. It is connected to other processes through which students learn and explore math ideas. The NCTM Process Standards (2000) of problem solving, communication, representation, reasoning and proof, and connections describe critical processes that are intertwined in our math lessons. While solving problems, students communicate verbally and in writing in order to process and express their ideas. They decipher representations to understand problem data or create representations to show their thinking. They use reasoning skills to inference, draw conclusions, and justify their solutions. They connect various math ideas in order to better understand each one, and they connect math to their lives as they explore problems in a real-world context. These five process standards interconnect in daily lessons as we develop and refine math content with our students.

While there is much overlap between the process standards, there must also be a strong connection between the process and content standards. Problem solving is a process through which students learn math content and through which they are able to apply their math skills. Providing students with experiences solving problems in various content areas is a critical way to help students practice application of these skills as well as actively engaging them with math content. The National Council of Teachers of Mathematics (2000) has outlined the content standards for elementary students and has organized those standards in five content areas: number and operations, algebra, measurement, geometry, and data analysis and probability. While we help students develop their skills in the processes of problem solving, reasoning and proof, communication, representation, and connections, we are also focused on building their understanding of this content. This chapter explores the interconnectedness of the content and process standards through sample activities that illustrate a blending of content and process. Classroom activities are highlighted to illustrate problem solving in each content area. The activities are directly linked to the NCTM standards and expectations for students in grades 3 through 5 (NCTM 2000). Resources to support you in implementing these activities are available on the accompanying CD.

Problem Solving About Number and Operations

In grades 3 through 5, students are exploring various ways of representing numbers. They are developing their understanding of fractions both as parts of a whole or a collection and as division of whole numbers. They are continuing their study of operations and developing their understanding of multiplication and division, as well as increasing their skills at choosing appropriate operations to solve problems. The following activity challenges students to use their understanding of fractions, their knowledge of operations, their computation abilities, and their problem-solving skills to find a reasonable solution to the problem.

The Problem Task

The following problem was posed in a third-grade classroom in order to observe students' ideas about numbers and operations as well as to provide an opportunity to expand their understandings. Through this problem task, students were immediately engaged in exploring math content through the process of problem solving.

> Danny's mother made cookies for his party. She made 36 cookies. The girls ate $\frac{1}{4}$ of them. The boys ate $\frac{1}{3}$ of them. If the 10 parents at the party shared the rest equally, how many cookies did each parent get?

In order to promote discussion about their thinking, third-grade students were asked to work in pairs to solve this problem. The teacher, Ms. Dennis, posed the problem and clarified the task, asking students to solve the problem with their partners and to record their work, solutions, and explanations of how they solved the problem. Students had access to materials including colored disks, paper, and pencils. Ms. Dennis moved through the room to monitor and support students as they worked (a benefit of partner and group work as the teacher is free to move to different groups and question or support them as needed).

A first step for many students was to visualize the problem situation. Students created a variety of pictures or diagrams to represent the 36 cookies ranging from diagrams in which students drew each cookie (including the chocolate chips!) to pictures in which the cookies were represented by x's, circles, or c's. Many students began to circle $\frac{1}{4}$ of the cookies and label the group as "girls," and then circle $\frac{1}{3}$ of the cookies and label them as "boys." The students were then able to use their diagrams to determine the remaining cookies which were identified as "parents" simply by counting the cookies that had not been circled.

After determining the number of cookies eaten by the girls, boys, and parents, the students still needed to determine how many cookies each parent would receive. Of course, the parents could not share the remaining 15 cookies equally unless fractional parts were considered. Several pairs quickly responded that the parents would get one cookie each and that there would be 5 cookies left over, hoping that could be the answer. While that observation showed a good understanding of numbers, they were reminded by Ms. Dennis that all 15 of the remaining cookies must be shared equally by the 10 parents. In many pairs, discussions between partners led them to the conclusion that parents would get $1\frac{1}{2}$ cookies each as they recognized the relationship between the 5 remaining cookies and the 10 parents. Shauna remarked, "Hey after they all get one, there's half as many cookies still left—they could each share a cookie with someone else!" However, some students still needed to picture the information in order to formulate their conclusion. After some initial confusion, actually drawing and "cutting" cookies in half led several pairs to the conclusion that each parent would get $1\frac{1}{2}$ cookies.

One student, Alex, motioned to Ms. Dennis and told her that he didn't need a picture—that he already knew the answer. Ms. Dennis asked him to tell her how he would solve the problem. Alex, an abstract thinker, explained his process:

"I knew the girls got 9 cookies each because $4 \times \underline{9} = 36$ and I knew the boys got 12 cookies because $3 \times \underline{12} = 36$. Each parent gets $1\frac{1}{2}$ cookies because $1\frac{1}{2} + 1\frac{1}{2} + 1\frac{1}{2} + 1\frac{1}{2} + 1\frac{1}{2} + 1\frac{1}{2} + 1\frac{1}{2} + 1\frac{1}{2} + 1\frac{1}{2} + 1\frac{1}{2} = 15$ and there are 15 cookies left."

While other students found the pictures invaluable, Alex was able to move through the problem without their help. He jumped right into calculations, understanding the need to find $\frac{1}{4}$ of 36 and $\frac{1}{3}$ of 36 (and knowing how the fractions connected to the operations of multiplication and division, that $\frac{1}{3}$ is like finding a missing factor as in $3 \times \square = 36$). He also recognized the need to add the answers to find the total eaten by the boys and girls, moving on to subtraction to find the total remaining for the parents ("I know the boys and girls had 21 because it's 9 and 12, so that makes 15 left because there are 36 altogether and you have to take 21 away."). He was even able to determine that 15 divided by 10 was $1\frac{1}{2}$ and had no calculations on his paper. After several questions to gather insights about his thinking, Ms. Dennis was able to determine that he immediately recognized that each parent could have one cookie and that with 5 still remaining, they would get another $\frac{1}{2}$ cookie each. Ms. Dennis encouraged him to record his method of solving the problem and he recorded his series of equations.

During partner work, Ms. Dennis asked a variety of questions to stimulate students' thoughts and redirect those who became blocked or frustrated. Jayson and Marcy struggled with their initial attempt at diagramming the problem. After being asked to explain their diagram to her, they recognized their error and demonstrated their persistence as they crossed out their first attempt and then began with a new diagram, and some new insights. Finally, they wrote "We know that the parents got $1\frac{1}{2}$ each because each got 1 but 5 were left so we broke them in 2 so each person also got half." They got it! Not as quickly as some others, but their understanding was genuine.

Ms. Dennis facilitated a sharing session to discuss ways in which students solved the problem. She selected several pairs to share their strategies, and recorded their ideas on the overhead as they spoke, drawing diagrams and recording the operations they performed. She then engaged students in a discussion of what was hard about the problem and how they made it easier. Students shared their frustration at trying to figure out how to equally share the remaining cookies, their success at using diagrams to find the fractional parts, and their delight at ultimately finding the answer.

About the Math

This problem challenged students to combine their understanding of numbers and operations with their problem-solving skills. In solving this problem, students used their understanding of fractions as they determined thirds and fourths of a collection (set). Some students demonstrated their understanding by drawing pictures to represent one-third or one-fourth of the collection, while others were able to apply their recognition of the link between fractions and division (and its inverse—multiplication) to determine important problem data. While those students who had relied on pictures simply counted the remaining cookies to find the number left for the parents, others showed their understanding of operations as they added to find the number of cookies eaten by the boys and girls together and then subtracted from the total to find the number left for the parents to share.

Once students determined that 15 cookies would be left to equally share between 10 parents, they were challenged to figure out a strategy to find how many cookies each parent would receive. Some students demonstrated their understanding of the fractional problem as they drew diagrams to "cut and share cookies" to create ten equal groups of $1\frac{1}{2}$ cookies. Others applied their understanding of operations as they subtracted 10 from the 15 cookies in order to give each parent one cookie, and then recognized that the 5 remaining cookies could be shared among 10 parents if each cookie was cut in half (a recognition of 10 being double 5).

As the teacher recorded students' ideas during the class sharing, students were able to see varied approaches to the fraction problem ranging from visually diagramming the problem to understanding how operations could lead to a solution. And students gained greater insight into fractions as they saw examples of fractions viewed as both equal sharing and division of whole numbers. And although the term *division with remainders* was not used in the lesson, students were exposed to the concept, providing a foundation for future math experiences.

As students strengthened their understanding of fractions and operations throughout this activity, they also refined their use of problem-solving strategies. Some students demonstrated their problem-solving skills as they created pictures and diagrams to simplify the problem, or chose a correct operation as they added, subtracted, multiplied, or divided to get their answers. They began to develop their skills at multistep problems as they proceeded through several steps in search of the answer. And they worked to enhance their problem-solving attitudes through persistence, despite some frustration, and cooperation with their partners as they worked together to share ideas and strategies.

This activity required students to pull from their understanding of fractions and operations to solve a multistep problem. While there were several effective methods for solving the problem, students had opportunities to hear each others' ideas and approaches in order to expand their repertoire of problem-solving skills and enhance their understanding of fractions. Some students applied an already developed understanding of fractions and operations to the problem, while others gained insights and continued to refine their understandings through the problem-solving task.

Problem Solving About Algebra

An important goal for students in grades 3 through 5 is the development of their understanding of patterns and functions. Students who can organize data so that they can recognize patterns or discover functional (change) relationships are better able to find solutions to problems. Analyzing change in various contexts is an important algebra skill as students observe change and attempt to determine how change in one variable relates to change in another. Describing this change and making generalizations about it are beneficial skills. In the following problem, students were challenged to model, record, observe, and generalize about patterns and functions.

The Problem Task

The teacher, Mrs. Millman, posed the following problem to her fourth-grade class:

> **Rockledge School had an ice cream social. The students and parents were seated at square tables. Only 1 person could sit at each side of a table. If 40 tables were pushed together into one long row of tables, how many people could be seated? Explain how you know.**

Mrs. Millman began this problem by exploring some data with the whole class. Students were asked how many people could be seated if 2 tables were pushed together. Students worked with partners and were given eight to ten square tiles to physically explore the task. Students pushed two square tiles (models for tables) together and counted the number of people who could sit on each side, identifying that 6 people could be seated at 2 connected square tables. Mrs. Millman then asked students to determine how many people could sit in a row of 3 connected tables. Again students used square tiles to determine that 8 people could be seated. Mrs. Millman then posed the problem asking how many people could be seated at 40 tables. Students seemed a bit confused as they did not have enough square tiles to create a model of the row of 40 tables. Mrs. Millman suggested that they might have (and be able to collect more) data that might help them figure out the solution.

Students worked in pairs to complete this task. Students began to gather data and most recorded the information they collected (although some pairs were not recording their data and benefited from a prompt from the teacher in the form of questions like "How are you going to remember what you've already done?" or "What data do you already have?"). Many pairs chose to create tables to show their data, although the tables varied, some being vertical, others horizontal. One pair simply recorded the various numbers of people who could be seated. After recording data, the students began to verbalize observations about their data. Some quickly generalized to figure out a rule or formula for calculating the area of longer rows (double the number of tables and add 2) (see Figure 14–1), while others continued to record data following an observed pattern, creating very lengthy data tables (see Figure 14–2).

As Mrs. Millman moved through the room to support students and observe their problem-solving skills, she noticed several pairs who began to quickly complete the tables with the data they thought would be on them rather than actually collecting data, observing for patterns, and then continuing the table using the observed pattern. Carefully selected questions helped slow these students down and pushed them to take a closer look at their data, resulting in some pairs deciding to start over with their data collection.

A whole-class sharing provided students with opportunities to share their strategies, defend their answers, and better understand the importance of looking for patterns and functions. While most students shared their observations about patterns, a couple of them shared an insight about a relationship between the number of tables and the number of people. Kyle said that if you add 1 to the number of tables and then doubled it, you would get the number of people. The class tried it with several

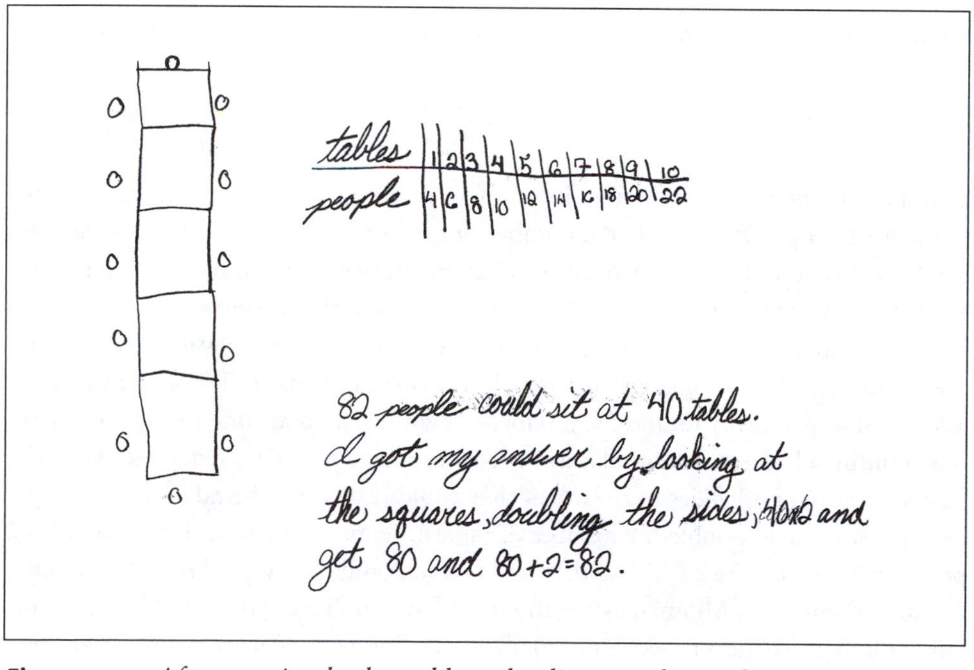

Figure 14–1 *After creating both a table and a diagram, this student recognized a functional relationship in the data (double the number of tables + 2).*

tables	people		tables	people
1	4		24	50
2	6		25	52
3	8		26	54
4	10		27	56
5	12		28	58
6	14		29	60
7	16		30	62
8	18		31	64
9	20		32	66
10	22		33	68
11	24		34	70
12	26		35	72
13	28		36	74
14	30		37	76
15	32		38	78
16	34		39	80
17	36		40	82
18	38			
19	40			
20	42			
21	44			
22	46			
23	48			

I know 82 people could sit at 40 tables because I saw a pattern that you add two each time you add a table.

Figure 14–2 *This student recognized a pattern and continued it to find a solution.*

examples on their table and found it to be true each time. Jordan mentioned that the number of people was double the number of tables plus 2 more and again the class tried it with examples from their tables. Once more, they found it to work every time. Students were asked why those rules, or as they called them "shortcuts," seemed to work each time. After some discussions with their partners, no one was able to explain the shortcuts. Mrs. Millman then put eight transparent square tiles on the overhead asking for a quick way to find the number of people seated around the squares without counting all the way around the long row of tables. Students suggested that since someone sat on both sides of the tables they could just count the tables and multiply by 2 (or some said double the number of tables). Jenna noted that there were also 2 people who sat on the 2 ends, so they had to add 2 and they would have the number for all of them. Mrs. Millman asked about Jordan's and Kyle's rules and had students talk with their partners to see if they made sense with the model on the overhead. Several pairs excitedly said that it was like the way we counted the tables as a shortcut (double the number was like doubling because someone sat on each side of the table and adding 2 was the 2 people on the ends). The teacher then asked if they could figure out how many people sat at a row of 100 tables or 1,000 tables and students quickly gave the answers. Mrs. Millman modeled writing the equations on the board, $(8 \times 2) + 2 = 18$ or $(100 \times 2) + 2 = 202$, as students described how they might quickly find the answers. She asked the students to talk with their partners about how knowing that rule, or shortcut, would help them solve problems. Students were able to verbalize that while continuing the pattern might get them to the answer, the rule that they found from looking at the relationship between the number of tables and people (the functional relationship) would allow them to get answers to tough problems (e.g., How many people sat at 1,000 tables?) and to get the answers more quickly. The students were learning that while several strategies may help them find an answer, some can be more efficient than others.

About the Math

Modeling problem situations with manipulatives, using tables to record the data gathered, and drawing conclusions from the data are important skills for intermediate students. A major focus of this task was the recognition and understanding of patterns and functions in the data that was collected. Rather than collecting data for all 40 tables, a recognition of patterns and functions allowed students to formulate rules or generalizations based on the collection of a limited amount of data. And modeling ways to express the math relationships using equations began to build important foundations for algebra.

Varied problem-solving strategies were noted during this task. While most students used physical objects (square tiles) to help with the collection of data, others used pictures or diagrams of the rows of tables to begin to generate their data. Students refined their skill of organizing data in order to better view and analyze (through creating tables), and refined their abilities to see and describe patterns and functions as they justified and described their observations to their partners and the whole class.

This problem-solving task focused on extending both students' understanding of patterns and functions, as well as enhancing their abilities to record and organize data to allow for greater insights into the relationships between the data. Exploring ideas in a problem context engaged students and set the stage for student discovery about rules and generalizations that serve as shortcuts to finding the solution to more complex problems!

Problem Solving About Measurement

Students in grades 3 through 5 are expected to understand measurement attributes including length and width. In the intermediate grades, they are developing their understanding of ways to determine the area and perimeter of shapes and are becoming familiar with formulas and how to apply the formulas to calculate area and perimeter.

It is critical at this level that students recognize the concepts of area and perimeter in problem situations. In the following problem, students were challenged to demonstrate their understanding of area and perimeter as well as their ability to correctly calculate each.

The Problem Task

> **Ellen and her mother are shopping for supplies for their new flower garden. They need to buy enough flower seeds for the rectangular garden that measures 10 feet wide and 15 feet long. The directions on the seed packets say to buy a packet of seeds for every 10 square feet in the garden. How many packets of flower seeds will they need to buy?**
>
> **While at the store, they find a fancy white border to place around their flower garden. How many feet of border will they need to buy?**

Fifth-grade students explored this multistep problem task. Students worked with partners to explore the problem. They were asked to solve the problem and then to write about their solutions with the following prompt:

> **Ellen's brother does not agree with your answers. He says it will not be enough flower seeds or fencing. Convince him that your answers are correct.**

A few students dove into the problem with a quick application of formulas for area and perimeter, but most students first drew a diagram of the garden, labeled it, and used it to guide their thinking. Partners were often overheard clarifying area and perimeter. The teacher, Miss Hosty, did not contribute to the discussions unless frustration was evident between both partners, allowing first an opportunity for partners to guide each other. Students often needed to discuss the situation (e.g., seeds for the garden) to determine if area or perimeter made sense. Miss Hosty joined several discussions as partners worked to clarify their understanding of the questions being asked. She listened and posed additional questions as needed (i.e., So, why does it matter if a seed packet covers 10 square feet? So how does that help you?).

Miss Hosty joined one group of students who were struggling with their understandings. She separated the tasks and had them focus on one task at a time, providing them with support through her questions. She provided hints to help them connect the task to similar classroom activities in order to help them distinguish between the area and perimeter concepts. Once students saw the connections with familiar tasks, they were able to continue on their own, allowing Miss Hosty to move to another group.

Another group quickly finished the problem. As Miss Hosty joined them, she asked them to explain their work to her, which they were easily able to do. She then posed an extension problem to this group: *Ellen's friend, Lily, also wanted to plant a flower garden. Lily had a square garden with a perimeter of 120 feet. How much border and how many seed packets would she need?* She waited for a moment to hear the beginning of discussions on how they might find the answers, noticing some initial confusion about not having any length or width measurements for the garden. This problem required students to use the only information they had (perimeter = 120 feet) and their recognition that the garden was square to determine that each side must measure 30 feet. That data could then be used to continue solving the problem. Students began to discuss how to get started and Miss Hosty, satisfied that they could proceed with the discussions, moved on to another group. The ability to move in and out of groups, provided the teacher with opportunities to differentiate instruction by supporting struggling students and challenging those who would benefit from a more complex task.

Finding the solutions was easier for many students than writing their convincing arguments as to why their solutions were correct. Miss Hosty needed to prompt many students with questions like "How many flower seed packets will you need? Tell me why you believe that is right. How can you be sure?" to jump-start their communication about their approaches and solutions. She noticed that several pairs were better able to write their ideas after verbalizing their ideas. She suggested to partners that they might want to first tell each other why they believe their answers were correct before writing down their ideas. Through their justifications, Miss Hosty was able to gain better insight into their thinking. Joy wrote, "We will have enough because to find the area you multiply length by width (15 ft. × 10 ft. = 150 sq. ft.). Then 1 packet is for every 10 sq. ft. so you divide 150 by 10 so you know you need 15 packets for the whole garden because 15 packets × 10 square feet is 150 square feet and that's the area. To make sure we have enough fencing we just add all the sides so 10 ft. + 10 ft. + 15 ft. + 15 ft. = 50 ft. It's just like finding the perimeter!" Other students supported their answers with diagrams, representations of their calculations, and written justifications (see Figure 14–3).

About the Math

This task required students to recognize that determining the area and perimeter of the garden were essential steps to solving the problem. Students had to calculate the perimeter and recognize that the measurement indicated the length of fencing needed to go around all sides of the garden. In addition, they had to calculate the area of the garden and use that measurement to determine the number of 10 square foot sections that were in the total area in order to find the number of seed packets that were needed. In determining the measurements, students had to apply their computation skills as they added, multiplied, and divided to find the answers.

Problem-solving skills were also critical. Many students needed to picture the problem situation and began with a diagram of the garden. After labeling the diagram with the measurements, students were better able to visualize and continue the task. Students also recognized and applied formulas to the problem situation. And this problem provided students with practice in working through multistep tasks as they were required to determine both area and perimeter before completing the task. The extension task posed to the group who finished quickly required students to use a work backward approach, starting with the knowledge of the perimeter to then determine

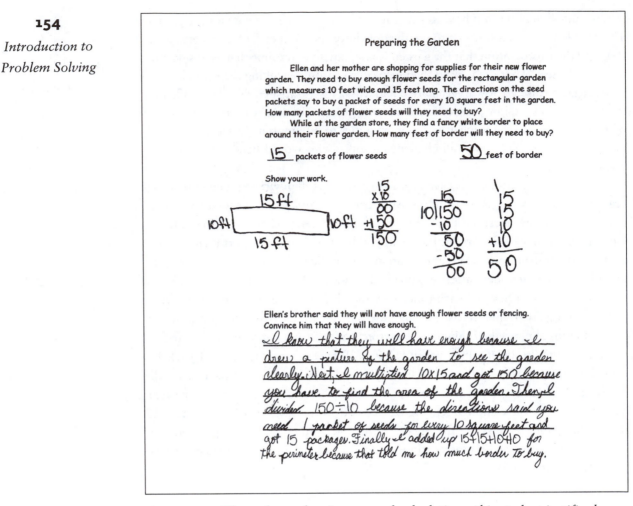

Figure 14–3 *Through words, pictures, and calculations, this student justifies her solutions to the problem.*

the length of the garden sides. Through this problem exploration, students had opportunities to test and refine their understandings of area and perimeter measurement, as well as practice their computation skills and hone their problem-solving skills.

Problem Solving About Geometry

Students in grades 3 through 5 are building an understanding of transformations. They are developing their skills at being able to visualize the results of flipping, sliding, and turning figures. Recognizing congruent figures after transformations can be challenging for students at this level. Identifying line symmetry in two-dimensional shapes is also a geometry objective for intermediate students. The following task explores important geometry concepts such as congruency, transformations, and symmetry. Students are challenged to use their problem-solving skills to organize and simplify the process of finding all of the possible pentominoes, and then classifying the pentominoes based on line symmetry.

The Problem Task

Mr. Amos began this task by introducing dominoes and triominoes to his fifth-grade class, sharing examples of each. He then asked what a pentomino might be. Several students stated it would be a figure made from 4 squares, but many chimed in that it would have 5 squares. Mr. Amos asked what clues led them to believe it had 5 squares and several students responded that it was like "pentagon" with 5 sides. He then posed the following question to the class:

How many different pentominoes are possible?

Mr. Amos created an example on the board using large squares as models. The example showed a pentomino created by 5 squares in a row.

He emphasized the way in which the squares touched with sides connecting to each other and shared an example and nonexample as such:

Allowed   Not allowed

Mr. Amos then shared the following examples and asked if they were the same or different pentominoes.

Students were asked to discuss the question with a partner and then asked to share their ideas with the class. Most students agreed that the examples were not two different pentominoes, but one pentomino that had been flipped. Mr. Amos asked a student to demonstrate by flipping a cutout of the shape to verify students' ideas. He reminded students that their goal was to find all of the *different* pentominoes, so to be sure to flip and turn the pentominoes to ensure that they were different from others they had found.

Students were given square tiles, grid paper, and scissors, and were paired with a partner or placed in a group of three students and asked to find and cut out all of the possible pentominoes (see Figure 14–4). Many students began by experimenting with the square tiles and then cutting out pentominoes they had created with the models. Others began to outline pentominoes on the grid paper. Students found several possibilities very quickly, but began to debate and discuss with their partners as they searched for additional possibilities. As Mr. Amos moved through the room, he observed students flipping and turning the pentominoes as they checked to be sure they were unique. Many pairs found that two cutouts were congruent after playing with transformations, and discarded one of the cutouts.

As students continued to work on finding more possibilities, several groups began to line up their pentominoes across their desks, looking for a pattern or way

Figure 14–4 *These students are actively involved in finding possible pentominoes.*

to organize them. One group began with the pentomino of 5 squares in a row and then placed any pentominoes that had 4 squares in a row, then 3 squares in a row, trying to search for any possibilities they might have missed.

When students thought they had all of the possibilities, they were asked to compare their pentominoes with the group sitting across from them. While several groups found the 12 possibilities, other groups were assisted by sharing ideas with another team and seeing formations that were missed. When all groups had completed the task, students were asked to share some insights. Some comments included that the first pentominoes they made were easy but that it got harder as they went on, that they were glad they could cut them out and flip and turn them, that lining them up in an order helped them figure out a missing arrangement, and that working with a partner helped them think of more ways to arrange the squares.

Mr. Amos then asked students to sort the pentominoes based on whether they had a line of symmetry. Students were given large white paper and asked to fold it in half and label the sides "symmetry" and "no symmetry," and then to decide where each pentomino should be placed. Students were also asked to find any lines of symmetry and to draw the lines of symmetry on the pentominoes, finally gluing each pentomino on the correct side of their charts.

Students began folding, sorting, and drawing lines of symmetry quickly for some shapes and more slowly for others. After partners sorted, they verified their work through discussions with the other pair at their table.

Mr. Amos then asked students to tape their charts to the board so the completed charts could be reviewed and discussed. The students commented that having the pentominoes cut out, so they could fold them to check for symmetry, helped them, especially when partners disagreed. Several students verbalized their surprise about which pentominoes had lines of symmetry, noting that some had a line of symmetry, or several, even though it didn't initially seem as though they would.

About the Math

This task required students to create pentominoes and check their uniqueness based on an understanding of transformations. Students flipped and turned pentominoes to ensure that they were unique (not congruent figures that had been flipped or turned), sometimes verifying their predictions and sometimes finding surprises along the way. Students explored the concept of line symmetry using physical models that could be folded to test their predictions. While obvious lines of symmetry were quick for students to identify, some lines of symmetry were more difficult for them to recognize (see Figure 14–5). Sharing the ideas between teams, and as a whole class, allowed them to identify a greater number of lines of symmetry.

Figure 14–5 *Students marked pentominoes showing the lines of symmetry that were identified.*

To solve this problem, students used both physical models and drawings. Both helped them visualize the ideas. And several groups, when frustrated in their ability to find more pentominoes, resorted to organizing their pentominoes into lists beginning with 5 squares in a row, then 4 squares in a row, then 3. Organizing them in that way helped them recognize several pentominoes that they had missed. Their organization skills and ability to visualize the task through models and diagrams supported their ability to find the solutions. And persistence was an essential ingredient to success in this activity. While students found it easy to create the first few pentominoes, the task got increasingly difficult, and sometimes frustrating, as they inched closer to finding all of the possibilities.

Problem Solving About Data and Probability

Intermediate students are developing an understanding of basic probability concepts. Students in grades 3 through 5 are learning to describe events using probability terms like *unlikely, likely,* and *equally likely,* as well as expressing probability using a numeric representation between 0 and 1. They are developing their skills at conducting probability investigations, as well as developing an understanding of the difference between theoretical and experimental probability. The following activity requires students to gather data and then express the probability of events in a problem situation.

The Problem Task

> Visitors at the county fair had a chance to win a prize by spinning 2 prize wheels. One wheel displayed the numbers 1–4; the other wheel displayed the numbers 5–8. Each person was able to spin each wheel one time and then asked to find the product of the two spins. If the product was greater than 15, the visitor won a free lemonade. If the product was greater than 25, the visitor also won a free popcorn.

A fourth-grade teacher, Mrs. O'Connor, began the task by explaining the situation and asking her students if they thought they would win a prize. Students had various comments, some indicating that they thought they would win and others saying they did not think so. Mrs. O'Connor suggested that they gather some data. Each pair was given a spinner and asked to spin each wheel once (see Figure 14–6). Students were then asked to find the product of their two numbers and decide whether they would win. After a few minutes, one student asked, "Does 15 win a prize?" The teacher restated the question "Does 15 win a prize?" and asked them to talk it over with their partners. Mrs. O'Connor asked for students to indicate their decision with a show of hands. One pair indicated that it would win, but the others indicated it wouldn't. She asked for arguments to defend their answers. Several students explained that it would not win because 15 is not greater than 15 (emphasizing the word *greater*). The students who had initially decided that 15 would win smiled and nodded, understanding the explanation. Mrs. O'Connor told students to talk with their partners and decide if 25 would win a free lemonade and popcorn, and then listened to student discus-

Figure 14–6 *Students test their predictions about winning prizes
by spinning the wheels.*

sions to be sure that students got the idea. Students then went back to work to determine their product and what they would win.

Mrs. O'Connor placed a chart on the wall to record their results. Each pair indicated whether they won nothing, a lemonade, or a lemonade and popcorn, and Mrs.
O'Connor placed the appropriate mark on the chart. Some students were observed
spinning several times to try to get a product greater than 15 (a very typical reaction
at this level). Mrs. O'Connor reminded students that the goal of the activity was to
figure out the *chance* of winning a prize. She assured them that it did not matter if
they won a prize (they would not actually be getting the lemonade or popcorn!), but
that they were doing this to get an idea of what their chances really were for getting
a prize.

After data was recorded on the chart for two spins for each student, Mrs. O'Connor asked what the probability was for winning a lemonade. Students were asked to
talk it over with their partners. While some pairs looked to the chart for the answer,
others suggested that wasn't the "real probability" and that they would need to know
how many products were greater than 15 to figure it out. While some students had a
sense for the data that needed to be collected, others looked confused. The teacher decided to discuss a simpler example that had been done in class. She asked, "What is
the probability that I will roll a 4 when I roll a number cube?" Students agreed that it
was $\frac{1}{6}$. Mrs. O'Connor asked them to explain to her what the 1 and 6 represented.
Students explained that there was only one 4 on a number cube, but there were 6
numbers on the cube, so the chance was $\frac{1}{6}$ of rolling a 4. She then asked them the

probability of rolling a 5. They agreed it was $\frac{1}{6}$ and again justified their answer. Mrs. O'Connor asked what information they would need in order to find the probability of getting a free lemonade. Students were asked to discuss this with their partners and then share their ideas with the class. The students now recognized that they needed to know how many products were possible and how many of them were greater than 15.

The students worked together to determine all of the possible number pairs when both wheels were spun. Students recorded the combinations in several different ways. The students had prior experience solving simple organized list problems and most of them moved through the data in an organized manner, beginning with one number and exhausting all of the possibilities from the other wheel. A couple pairs began listing random pairs and did not find them all. Mrs. O'Connor asked them guiding questions "Are you sure you got all of the possibilities? Did you miss any? How can you be sure?"

As Mrs. O'Connor circulated through the room observing students at work, she noticed some interesting points and asked several pairs to share their ideas with the class. Kyle and Keira showed the group how they shaded each number on the first wheel after they matched it with all of the numbers on the second wheel. They said that helped them know which numbers they already did. Josh and Emily also had a system to help them remember which combinations had been done, using checkmarks as they completed each number on the first wheel. Doreen and Joseph then shared their recording of the combinations and their insights about the patterns they discovered (i.e., 1×5, 1×6, 1×7, 1×8 had products of 5, 6, 7, 8 and 2×5, 2×6, 2×7, 2×8 had products of 10, 12, 14, 16). Noticing the patterns that were formed as they looked for all of the combinations helped them have confidence in their answer—there were definitely 16 number combinations!

After the students shared their strategies and insights for finding the possible number combinations and the products, Mrs. O'Connor then returned to the initial problem:

> **The sign by the prize wheels says:**
> **Spin both wheels.**
> **If the product is greater than 15, you win a free lemonade.**
> **If the product is greater than 25, you win a free lemonade and a free popcorn.**
> **What is the probability of winning a free lemonade? What is the probability of winning both a free lemonade and a free popcorn?**

Partners worked together to find the probabilities and to explain, in writing, how they figured them out. The teacher then asked each pair to share their solutions with the pair sitting near them to see if they agreed. If they disagreed, they were asked to discuss the probabilities and decide on the correct probabilities. If they could not decide, they were asked to raise their hands so the teacher could come to assist them.

As the students worked on calculating the probabilities, Mrs. O'Connor noticed that a couple pairs were finished. After hearing their explanations, she produced a different wheel. This one had five numbers on it (5, 6, 7, 8, 9). "What if the second wheel had looked like this?" she said. "Would that change the probabilities of getting a prize? How?" The students began working on the extended task.

Following the task, Mrs. O'Connor facilitated a whole-group discussion to share the probabilities, asking students to justify their answers. Lindsay reported that the probability of winning a lemonade and a popcorn was $\frac{2}{16}$: "I found my answer by finding all the possible outcomes of getting 25 or greater and found 2 and that's my numerator. Just $4 \times 7 = 28$ and $4 \times 8 = 32$ win. The 16 was the number of outcomes in all and that's my denominator." Other students also shared their thinking. The group of students that explored the extended task discussed their ideas with the class and everyone agreed they would like the spinner with 5 numbers because they would be more likely to win a lemonade and popcorn!

About the Math

In this task, students had opportunities to explore a variety of probability concepts. Early in the task, their understanding of the difference between theoretical and experimental probability was tested. Some students looked to the chart recording their class spins and needed to be reminded that probability is the likelihood of something happening even if it does not always happen that way.

In order to determine the probabilities for winning prizes, students had to understand the concept of probability and know that they needed to find the number of possible outcomes that fit a criteria (e.g., number of products greater than 15) and the total number of outcomes (e.g., all of the number pairs possible when spinning the two wheels). Students were also required to understand how to represent probability in fractional form. An understanding of numerators and denominators, as well as what each represents, was critical for them to accurately create a fraction to represent their data. Students were also required to use their computation skills (multiplication) to determine the possible products.

In solving this problem, many students applied their understanding of organized lists. As they worked to determine the possible number pairs (and products), many students began with a number on the first wheel and exhausted combinations with each number on the second wheel before moving on. This systematic approach helped the students keep track of their work and, at least for one group, revealed patterns that assured them that their answers made sense.

This task also challenged students' understanding of math vocabulary. Terms like *product, likely, chance, greater than, probability, numerator,* and *denominator* were vital to the task. To complete this multistep activity, students were required to blend their understanding of probability, fractions, multiplication, and the problem-solving skill of organized lists. Throughout the task, they were supported by teacher questioning and benefited from the ability to talk and work with their peers.

Linking Problem Solving and Math Content

Problem-solving activities provide students with opportunities to explore math content and expand their understanding of that content, to apply math skills to problem situations, and to practice their use of problem-solving strategies. Whether problems focus on numbers and operations, algebra, geometry, measurement, or data and probability, students benefit from opportunities to explore math content through problems. When problem-solving tasks are carefully selected, they serve to expand and refine students' understanding of the problem-solving process as well as their understanding of math content.

Questions for Discussion

1. How are problem-solving skills reinforced during these tasks?

2. What should the teacher consider when selecting problem tasks? What considerations during planning would result in more effective problem-solving lessons?

3. How does integrating content and process enhance student learning?

4. In what ways should teachers support students as they engage in problem-solving lessons?

5. How might the teacher support struggling students and challenge gifted students during problem tasks?

Accepting the Challenge

Teaching mathematics well is a complex endeavor; and there are no easy recipes.

—National Council of Teachers of Mathematics,
Principles and Standards for School Mathematics

Teaching students to become effective problem solvers is both the goal and the challenge of elementary mathematics instruction. The goal is for students to solve problems, not to perform isolated math drills. Through the process of solving problems, students recognize the meaningfulness of the math we teach, identify ways to apply math skills to find solutions to problems, and gain greater insight into the mathematics they are exploring. Problem solving engages students in the study of mathematics. It motivates them, stimulates their curiosity, and helps them gain insights.

But problem solving is challenging for our students as it requires them to understand math skills and concepts, and to develop the thinking skills necessary to apply those skills and concepts to problem situations. Problem solving is not something that can be memorized. Each problem task requires thought, discussion, planning, and an understanding of which math skills to apply and how to apply them to solve the problem.

We are beginning to recognize the importance of teaching through problem solving, of allowing students to explore math ideas through problem tasks. And we are recognizing the importance of focusing on the teaching of problem-solving skills to support students as they develop a repertoire of strategies for approaching problems. We have identified skills and strategies that guide students through the problem-solving process and assist them in organizing needed data. Discussions, group work, and writing in mathematics class have allowed students to share their thinking processes and

163

strengthen their understanding of the skills they are acquiring. And the integration of real-world data into the math classroom has challenged students to apply problem-solving skills to real situations.

Working Together to Build Effective Problem Solvers

Students benefit from ongoing experiences with problem solving, and schools that work together to support students' problem-solving skills are able to offer students the consistency of a problem-solving focus across grade levels. When students explore math through problem tasks and discuss their problem-solving skills from year to year, they are able to build on prior experiences and refine their understandings. It is both our individual responsibility, as well as a school responsibility, to develop our students' problem-solving skills, refine our teaching skills, and provide the most appropriate math education for our students.

Working to Refine Our Skills

Many of us had minimal experience with math problem solving when we were students in the math classroom. Many adults report that they rarely discussed problems, were not taught strategies, learned math skills in isolation, and focused on computations rather than problem solving. While we recognize the importance of problem solving and the need to support our students with problem-solving experiences, it can be challenging to change instructional approaches that are deeply rooted in our own past experiences. And to attempt the change on our own can be daunting. In many schools, teachers are recognizing the benefits of working together to develop a model of an effective teacher of math problem solving. Through co-planning, lesson sharing, professional development sessions, and teacher study groups, we are supporting each other as we develop our skills at teaching math problem solving.

Many teachers applaud the benefits of working in teams. Grade level, or other planning teams, provide teachers with an opportunity to discuss and co-plan instructional activities with colleagues. Team meetings offer a chance to share resources (e.g., materials, lesson plans), or provide a forum to generate lesson ideas. Teachers can work together to develop a problem task to set a context for an upcoming math concept, analyze samples of student work with colleagues, or debrief after problem experiences to share successes and brainstorm ways to avoid difficulties or clarify misunderstandings. Teaming, whether formal or informal, allows us to share ideas, refine our understandings, and grow as teachers.

The Role of the Administrator

The school or district administrator plays a key role in the development of teachers' skills. Providing ongoing professional development is a critical responsibility of administrators. Professional development comes in many shapes and sizes. Teachers benefit from workshops on problem-solving approaches in which new ideas are shared or teaching techniques are modeled. Workshops can infuse new ideas into a staff and are most valuable when there are several sessions, each building upon the others, and allowing for teacher reflection. Many schools support the viewing of videotaped classroom lessons (either commercial products or informal tapes made within the school) to provide teachers with examples of teaching methods and to stimulate discussion about the techniques and activities presented in the videotaped lessons. Videos allow teachers to view teaching techniques in action.

Faculty study groups have become a very popular form of professional development because of their ongoing format as well as their potential for encouraging reflection about practice. Study groups might take the form of book studies in which teachers select a relevant piece of professional literature to read and discuss with colleagues over a series of meetings, or might simply be groups of teachers that explore a component of instruction (e.g., math problem solving). A group facilitator guides the discussions and encourages teachers to try related activities in their classrooms, bring student work samples to sessions, or share reflections based on their own practice. Study groups place value on teachers' experiences and enhance those experiences through readings and subsequent discussions. Study groups sometimes evolve into inquiry groups in which teachers explore a key question about problem solving or action research groups in which they gather data and discuss their findings.

The school administrator has the ability to set priorities within the building. Through observations of teaching practice, the administrator can monitor and enhance teaching behaviors. Through the selection of topics for faculty meetings or professional development sessions, administrators can show the importance of math problem solving. Through the designation of a school-based math leader, specialist, or coach, administrators can be reassured that math goals will remain a priority and faculty will receive support and encouragement as they work to refine their skills. Through providing opportunities for discussions with colleagues, peer observations, and study groups, administrators can continue to enhance teacher effectiveness.

Meeting the Needs of All Students

Working together in a schoolwide effort to enhance students' problem-solving skills requires attention to all students within the school. Discussions should focus on ways to support struggling students, as well as strategies for extending the problem-solving skills of gifted students. Resource teachers and specialists play a key role in schoolwide growth. Specialists with expertise in gifted education, learning disabilities, or English language learners can provide valuable insights into ways to modify instruction to meet the specific needs of these students. Having all faculty assembled to discuss possible strategies will allow the specialist to offer tips based on their specific knowledge.

Differentiating instruction to meet the needs of all students is critical in the teaching of problem solving. Understanding key thinking skills and problem-solving strategies, and the way these strategies develop from simple to more complex, is fundamental knowledge that allows us to differentiate our instruction. As we observe students' skills and determine their level of understanding, knowledge of the progression of problem-solving skills will allow us to present simpler problems for students who need to develop foundation skills or extend problems for those who are ready to be challenged.

The Challenge to Educators

The NCTM Problem-Solving Process Standard guides our efforts to redefine our classroom instruction. As the central focus of the mathematics curriculum (NCTM 1989), problem solving deserves focus and attention within our classrooms, and problem-solving experiences must become a part of our daily mathematics practices. Through the development of a positive classroom climate, we allow our students to test their skills and extend their thinking in a safe, comfortable environment that supports risk taking and creative thinking. Through hands-on and visual teaching techniques, we enable our students to explore problem solving and begin to build a repertoire of strategies and skills to allow them to tackle even complex problems. Through think-aloud techniques, we share our thinking to allow students to see into our heads as they try to understand how to think like problem solvers. Through group and partner work, we allow students to verbalize their ideas, hear the ideas of others, and build on their understanding as they consider new ideas. Through a variety of practice activities, our students are able to extend and refine their skills. Through the introduction of real-world activities, we give our students opportunities to apply their knowledge to meaningful tasks. And through opportunities for students to identify and assess their own thinking strategies (metacognition), we show students the power of understanding their own thinking.

The National Council of Teachers of Mathematics, through their *Principles and Standards* (2000), has provided us with a guide to help our students develop as math problem solvers. Through an understanding of the problem-solving process standard, as well as an understanding of how it relates to the content standards, we can effectively integrate our teaching of math problem solving with our teaching of other math skills and concepts. We can support students to understand and apply their content skills and help them develop problem-solving strategies to solve a variety of math problems.

Our goal as math educators is to acquire skills and strategies to help our students grow as mathematical thinkers. We are challenged to experiment with new strategies and techniques within our classroom to allow students to visualize and experience problem-solving situations. We are challenged to encourage students to communicate their ideas, discuss alternate solutions, and monitor their own thinking processes. We are challenged to present new math ideas in problem contexts to allow students to build on their prior understandings through the active exploration of math concepts. We are challenged to stimulate students with thought-provoking, open-ended problems and guide our students toward reasonable solutions. We are challenged to connect students' classroom skills to meaningful real-world tasks, providing students with opportunities to apply their knowledge. We are challenged to create a classroom in which our students investigate, explore, reason, and communicate about problem solving on a daily basis and in which they can grow to become confident and capable problem solvers.

C L A S S R O O M - T E S T E D   T I P

Refining Our Instructional Practices

Our goal, as teachers, is to continue to strengthen our instructional skills to meet the changing needs of our students. To become an effective teacher of math problem solving, we are challenged to find ways to expand and refine our skills as we help students develop this critical math process. Try these activities to continue to refine your teaching skills:

- Read a piece of professional literature and reflect on it as you think about your own experiences in the classroom.

- Look carefully at your students' work. Look for evidence of what they know and clues for how you can help them improve their skills.

- Try new techniques and activities and then reflect on what you've tried. If they are not immediately successful, modify the activities, or your delivery of the activities, to find the best approach for your students.

- Find a colleague with whom you can discuss ideas, share experiences, or even observe his or her teaching.

- When planning math lessons, consider ways to incorporate problem-solving activities related to all content standards.

C L A S S R O O M - T E S T E D   T I P

Schoolwide Focus

Consider working together within your school to strengthen the problem-solving skills of students at all grade levels. Make problem solving a priority within your math classrooms. Try these schoolwide activities:

- Develop schoolwide programs to motivate students (e.g., Problem-of-the-Week announcements or schoolwide math challenges).

- Create a schoolwide problem-solving bulletin board to highlight exemplary samples of student work across all grade levels.

- Send problem-solving tips home in a parent newsletter or post them on a school website.

- Inventory supplies and manipulatives in your building and find a system for sharing them among colleagues.

- Hold a problem-solving family math night or discuss the importance of problem solving at your school's Back-to-School Night.

- Begin a problem-solving book study group or focus group for teachers in your school.

Questions for Discussion

1. What are the benefits of a schoolwide focus on math problem solving? How might you help to create a schoolwide focus?

2. In what ways can you improve your skills at teaching problem solving?

3. How does teaming support classroom teachers? In what ways can classroom teachers and specialists work together to support students as they learn to solve problems?

4. What is the role of the school administrator in developing teachers' understanding of the NCTM problem-solving standard? How might all teachers be supported to better understand the teaching of math problem solving?

Additional Resources for Problem Solving

The following resources are meant to support you as you continue to explore the problem-solving standard in grades 3 through 5. You will find a variety of text resources—books that will provide you with additional problem-solving activities or instructional strategies. A list of math websites is included to supply you with problem tasks, electronic manipulative ideas, or teacher resources. And for additional professional development, several video products are listed that allow you to view problem solving in classrooms and reflect on the video lessons whether alone or with a group of your colleagues.

Text Resources

The following text resources provide a variety of activities and strategies for supporting students as they develop their problem-solving skills:

AIMS. 1987. *Primarily Bears—Grades K–6*. Fresno, CA: AIMS Education Foundation.
Brumbaugh, D., L. Brumbaugh, and D. Rock. 2001. *Scratch Your Brain*. Pacific Grove, CA: Critical Thinking Books and Software.
Burns, M. 1982. *Math for Smarty Pants*. Boston: Little, Brown & Co.
———. 1987. *A Collection of Math Lessons from Grades 3 Through 6*. New York: Math Solutions.
———. 1992. *About Teaching Mathematics*. New York: Math Solutions.
Charles, R. I., and F. K. Lester Jr. 1985. *Problem Solving Experiences in Mathematics* (Grade 3). Palo Alto, CA: Dale Seymour Publications.
Charles, R. I., R. P. Mason, and G. Gallagher. 1985. *Problem Solving Experiences in Mathematics* (Grade 5). Palo Alto, CA: Dale Seymour Publications.
Charles, R. I., R. P. Mason, and L. Martin. 1985. *Problem Solving Experiences in Mathematics* (Grade 4). Palo Alto, CA: Dale Seymour Publications.
Charles, R. I., and E. A. Silver, eds. 1989. *The Teaching and Assessing of Mathematical Problem Solving*. Reston, VA: National Council of Teachers of Mathematics.

Coburn, T. G. 1993. *NCTM Addenda Series—Patterns*. Reston, VA: National Council of Teachers of Mathematics.

Hogeboom, S., and J. Goodnow. 1987. *The Problem Solver I Series*. Mountain View, CA: Creative Publications.

Lester, F. K., and R. I. Charles, eds. 2003. *Teaching Mathematics Through Problem Solving: Prekindergarten–Grade 6*. Reston, VA: National Council of Teachers of Mathematics.

Miller, E. 1998. *Read It! Draw It! Solve It!* Menlo Park, CA: Dale Seymour.

Nessel, D., and F. Newbold. 2003. *180 Think Aloud Math Word Problems*. New York: Scholastic.

National Council of Teachers of Mathematics. 1989. *Curriculum and Evaluation Standards for School Mathematics*. Reston, VA: National Council of Teachers of Mathematics.

———. 1991. *Professional Standards for Teaching Mathematics*. Reston, VA: National Council of Teachers of Mathematics.

———. 1995. *Assessment Standards for School Mathematics*. Reston, VA: National Council of Teachers of Mathematics.

———. 2000. *Principles and Standards for School Mathematics*. Reston, VA: National Council of Teachers of Mathematics.

———. 2006. *Curriculum Focal Points for Prekindergarten through Grade 8 Mathematics*. Reston, VA: National Council of Teachers of Mathematics.

O'Connell, S. R. 1998. *Real World Math for Grades 4–6*. Columbus, OH: Frank Schaffer Publications.

———. 2001. *Math—The Write Way*. 3 vols. Columbus, OH: Frank Schaffer Publications.

———. 2005. *Now I Get It: Strategies for Building Confident and Competent Mathematicians K–6*. Portsmouth, NH: Heinemann.

Post, B., and S. Eads. 1996. *Logic, Anyone?* Torrance, CA: Fearon Teacher Aids.

Sakshaug, L. E., M. Olson, and J. Olson. 2002. *Children Are Mathematical Problem Solvers*. Reston, VA: National Council of Teachers of Mathematics.

Schoenfield, M., and J. Rosenblatt. 1985. *Discovering Logic (Grades 4–6)*. Grand Rapids, MI: Fearon Teacher Aids.

———. 1985. *Playing with Logic (Grades 3–5)*. Grand Rapids, MI: Fearon Teacher Aids.

Stenmark, J. Kerr, ed. 1995. *101 Short Problems from EQUALS*. Berkeley, CA: Regents of the University of California.

Van de Walle, J., and L. H. Lovin. 2006. *Teaching Student-Centered Mathematics Grades 3–5*. New York: Pearson Education, Inc.

Westley, J. 1994. *Puddle Questions*. Mountain View, CA: Creative Publications.

Whitin, D. J., and R. Cox. 2003. *A Mathematical Passage: Strategies for Promoting Inquiry in Grades 4–6*. Portsmouth, NH: Heinemann.

Yeatts, K., M. Battista, S. Mayberry, D. Thompson, and J. Zawojewski. 2004. *Navigating Through Problem Solving and Reasoning in Grade 3*. Reston, VA: National Council of Teachers of Mathematics.

———. 2005. *Navigating Through Problem Solving and Reasoning in Grade 4*. Reston, VA: National Council of Teachers of Mathematics.

Web Resources

The following websites provide a variety of lesson ideas, classroom resources, and ready-to-use problem-solving tasks:

> **www.abcteach.com/directory/basics/math/problem_solving/**
> The abcteach website has problem solving activities from Pre-K through 8th grade. Some are free; others require site membership.

www.aimsedu.org/index.html

This AIMS (Activities Integrating Mathematics and Science) website includes sample activities, information on AIMS professional development, an online store, and other teacher resources.

www.eduplace.com/math/brain/index.html

This Houghton Mifflin website contains brain teasers for grades 3 through 8 as well as an archive of past problems.

www.etacuisenaire.com

This website of the ETA/Cuisenaire Company is a supplier of classroom mathematics manipulatives and teacher resource materials.

www.heinemann.com

This website of Heinemann Publishing Company is a source for a variety of professional development resources for teachers.

www.illuminations.nctm.org

Explore a variety of problem-based lessons on this website of the National Council of Teachers of Mathematics.

www.learner.org/channel/courses/teachingmath/grades3_5/session_03/index.html

This Annenberg Media site offers a free, self-paced online course to help teachers better understand the problem-solving standard including lesson excerpts, video clips, and reflection questions.

www.learningresources.com

This website of the Learning Resources Company is a source for a variety of mathematics manipulatives and teacher resource materials.

www.mathcats.com/storyproblems/housecat2.html

This website contains story problems written by students. Answers are scrambled, but appear when the cursor is moved across the screen.

www.math.com/teachers.html

This site offers lesson plans, classroom resources, links to "free stuff," problems of the week, worksheet generators, and online tutorial assistance.

http://mathforum.org/discussions/

This website offers a list of discussion forums by subject area. Teachers post problems or discussion topics so that others can reply with solutions or responses.

http://mathforum.org/funpow/

This Math Forum website offers an elementary problem of the week and a problem library. There is a fee to subscribe.

http://mathforum.org/mathmagic/

This website contains MathMagic posted challenges intended to motivate students to use computer technology while increasing problem-solving strategies and communication skills.

www.mathstories.com

The "House of Math Word Problems" contains problems at the elementary level in both English and Spanish. There is a fee to subscribe.

www.nctm.org

On this National Council of Teachers of Mathematics (NCTM) website you will find information on regional and national conferences sponsored by NCTM, as well as a variety of professional development materials.

www.tomsnyder.com
This Tom Snyder Productions website sells commercial problem-solving software
 products listed by grade level.
www.whitehouse.gov/kids/math/
This site offers White House Kids math challenges at elementary and middle
 school levels.
www.wits.ac.za/ssproule/pow.htm
This problem-of-the-week website lists links to problem-of-the-week sites at all
 academic levels and includes a site rating system.

Staff Development Training Videos

The following professional development training videos feature a problem-solving
focus for teaching mathematics and offer tips and strategies for the teaching of math
problem solving. These video programs allow teachers to view problem solving in action in intermediate-level classrooms and include manuals with reflection questions
and activity ideas.

*Increasing Students' Math Problem-Solving Skills Part I: Developing Core Problem-Solving
 Strategies, Grades 3–6.* 2004. Bellevue, WA: Bureau of Education and Research.
*Increasing Students' Math Problem-Solving Skills Part II: Expanding Students' Repertoire of
 Problem-Solving Strategies, Grades 3–6.* 2004. Bellevue, WA: Bureau of Education and
 Research.
Mathematics with Manipulatives. 1989. Vernon Hills, IL: ETA/Cuisenaire.

Bloomer, A. M., R. I. Charles, and F. K. Lester Jr. 1996. *Problem Solving Experiences in Mathematics* (Grade K). Menlo Park, CA: Addison-Wesley.

Brinker, L. 1998. "Using Recipes and Ratio Tables." *Teaching Children Mathematics* 5 (4): 218–24.

Burns, M. 1982. *Math for Smarty Pants*. Boston: Little, Brown & Co.

———. 1987. *A Collection of Math Lessons from Grades 3 Through 6*. New York: Math Solutions.

———. 1992. *About Teaching Mathematics*. New York: Math Solutions.

Campbell, P. 1997. "Connecting Instructional Practice to Student Thinking." *Teaching Children Mathematics* 4 (2): 106–10.

Carpenter, T. P., M. L. Franke, and L. Levi. 2003. *Thinking Mathematically*. Portsmouth, NH: Heinemann.

Chambers, D, ed. 2002. *Putting Research into Practice in the Elementary Grades*. Reston, VA: National Council of Teachers of Mathematics.

Charles, R. I., and F. K. Lester Jr. 1985. *Problem Solving Experiences in Mathematics* (Grade 3). Menlo Park, CA: Addison-Wesley.

Charles, R. I., F. K. Lester Jr., and A. Bloomer. 1996a. *Problem Solving Experiences in Mathematics* (Grade 1). Menlo Park, CA: Addison-Wesley.

———. 1996b. *Problem Solving Experiences in Mathematics* (Grade 2). Menlo Park, CA: Addison-Wesley.

Charles, R. I., R. P. Mason, and G. Gallagher. 1985. *Problem Solving Experiences in Mathematics* (Grade 5). Menlo Park, CA: Addison-Wesley.

Charles, R. I., R. P. Mason, and D. Garner. 1985. *Problem Solving Experiences in Mathematics* (Grade 6). Menlo Park, CA: Addison-Wesley.

Charles, R. I., R. P. Mason, and L. Martin. 1985. *Problem Solving Experiences in Mathematics* (Grade 4). Menlo Park, CA: Addison-Wesley.

Charles, R. I., and E. A. Silver, eds. 1989. *The Teaching and Assessing of Mathematical Problem Solving*. Reston, VA: National Council of Teachers of Mathematics.

Cobb, P., E. Yackel, T. Wood, G. Wheatley, and G. Merkel. 2002. "Creating a Problem-Solving Atmosphere." *Putting Research into Practice in the Elementary Grades*. Reston, VA: National Council of Teachers of Mathematics (pp. 72–74).

Coburn, T. G. 1993. *NCTM Addenda Series—Patterns*. Reston, VA: National Council of Teachers of Mathematics.

Economopoulis, K. 1998. "What Comes Next? The Mathematics of Pattern in Kindergarten." *Teaching Children Mathematics* 5 (4): 230–33.

English, L. 1992. "Problem Solving with Combinations." *Arithmetic Teacher* 40 (2): 72–77.

Ferrini-Mundy, J., G. Lappan, and E. Phillips. 1997. "Experiences with Patterning." *Teaching Children Mathematics* 3 (6): 282–88.

Forsten, C. 1992. *Teaching Thinking and Problem Solving in Math.* New York: Scholastic.

Giglio Andrews, A. 1997. "Doing What Comes Naturally: Talking About Mathematics." *Teaching Children Mathematics* 3 (5): 236–39.

Grouws, D. A., and T. L. Good. 2002. Issues in Problem-Solving Instruction. *Putting Reseach into Practice in the Elementary Grades.* Reston, VA: National Council of Teachers of Mathematics (pp. 60–62).

Hiebert, J. 1999. "Relationships Between Research and the NCTM Standards." *Journal for Research in Mathematics Education* 30 (1): 3–19.

Hiebert, J., T. Carpenter, E. Fennema, K. Fuson, D. Wearne, H. Murray, A. Olivier, and P. Human. 1997. *Making Sense: Teaching and Learning Mathematics with Understanding.* Portsmouth, NH: Heinemann.

Hogeboom, S., and J. Goodnow. 1987. *The Problem Solver I Series.* Mountain View, CA: Creative.

Johnson, D. R. 1994. *Motivation Counts—Teaching Techniques That Work.* Palo Alto, CA: Dale Seymour.

Kilpatrick, J., W. G. Martin, and D. Schifter, eds. 2003. *A Research Companion to Principles and Standards for School Mathematics.* Reston, VA: National Council of Teacher of Mathematics.

Kelly, J. A. 1999. "Improving Problem Solving through Drawings." *Teaching Children Mathematics* 6 (1): 48–51.

Kroll, D. L. , J. O. Masingila, and S. T. Mau. 1992. "Cooperative Problem Solving: But What About Grading?" *Arithmetic Teacher* 39 (6): 17–23.

Krulik, S., and J. A. Rudnick. 1994. "Reflect . . . for Better Problem Solving and Reasoning." *Arithmetic Teacher* 41 (6): 334–38.

Lester, F., and R. Charles, eds. 2003. *Teaching Mathematics Through Problem Solving: Prekindergarten–Grade 6.* Reston, VA: National Council of Teachers of Mathematics.

Meyer, C., and T. Sallee. 1983. *Make It Simpler: A Practical Guide to Problem Solving in Mathematics.* Menlo Park, CA: Addison-Wesley.

National Council of Teachers of Mathematics. 1989. *Curriculum and Evaluation Standards for School Mathematics.* Reston, VA: Author.

———. 1991. *Professional Standards for Teaching Mathematics.* Reston, VA: Author.

———. 1995. *Assessment Standards for School Mathematics.* Reston, VA: Author.

———. 2000. *Principles and Standards for School Mathematics.* Reston, VA: Author.

O'Connell, S. R. 1992. "Math Pairs—Parents as Partners." Arithmetic Teacher 40 (1): 10–12.

———. 1995. "Newspapers: Connecting the Mathematics Classroom to the World." *Teaching Children Mathematics* 1 (5): 268–74.

———. 1998. *Real World Math for Grades 4–6.* Columbus, OH: Frank Schaffer Publications.

———. 2001a. *Math—The Write Way for Grades 2–3.* Columbus, OH: Frank Schaffer Publications.

———. 2001b. *Math—The Write Way for Grades 4–5.* Columbus, OH: Frank Schaffer Publications.

———. 2005. *Now I Get It: Strategies for Building Confident and Competent Mathematicians K–6.* Portsmouth, NH: Heinemann.

———. 2007. *Introduction to Communication.* Portsmouth, NH: Heinemann.

O'Daffer, P. G., ed. 1988. *Problem Solving Tips for Teachers.* Reston, VA: National Council of Teachers of Mathematics.

Polya, G. 2004. *How To Solve It: A New Aspect of Mathematical Method,* 3rd ed. Princeton, NJ: Princeton University Press.

Post, B., and S. Eads. 1996. *Logic, Anyone?* Torrance, CA: Fearon Teacher Aids.

Reeves, C. A. 1987. *Problem-Solving Techniques Helpful in Mathematics and Science.* Reston, VA: National Council of Teachers of Mathematics.

Rowan, T., and B. Bourne. 2001. *Thinking Like Mathematicians.* Portsmouth, NH: Heinemann.

Schoenfield, M., and J. Rosenblatt. 1985a. *Discovering Logic.* Belmont, CA: David S. Lake.

———. 1985b. *Playing with Logic.* Belmont, CA: David S. Lake.

Shaw, J. M., M. S. Chambless, D. A. Chessin, V. Price, and G. Beardain. 1997. "Cooperative Problem Solving: Using K–W–D–L as an Organizational Technique." *Teaching Children Mathematics* 3 (9): 482–86.

Silver, E. A., and M. S. Smith. 2002. "Teaching Mathematics and Thinking." *Putting Research into Practice in the Elementary Grades.* Reston, VA: National Council of Teachers of Mathematics (pp. 63–67).

Smith, K. 1996. *Math Logic Puzzles.* New York: Sterling.

Sowder, L. 2002. "Story Problems and Students' Strategies." In *Putting Research into Practice in the Elementary Grades.* Reston, VA: National Council of Teachers of Mathematics (pp. 21–23).

Stenmark, J. K., ed. 1991. *Mathematics Assessment—Myths, Models, Good Questions, and Practical Suggestions.* Reston, VA: National Council of Teachers of Mathematics.

Van de Walle, J. A. 2004. *Elementary and Middle School Mathematics: Teaching Developmentally.* New York: Pearson Education.

Van de Walle, J. A., and L. H. Lovin. 2006. *Teaching Student-Centered Mathematics, Grades 3–5.* New York: Pearson Education.

Whitin, D., and R. Cox. 2003. *A Mathematical Passage: Strategies for Promoting Inquiry in Grades 4–6.* Portsmouth, NH: Heinemann.

Whitin, P., and D. Whitin. 2000. *Math Is Language Too: Talking and Writing in the Mathematics Classroom.* Urbana, IL: National Council of Teachers of English.

Yeatts, K., M. Battista, S. Mayberry, D. Thompson, and J. Zawojewski. 2004. *Navigating Through Problem Solving and Reasoning in Grade 3.* Reston, VA: National Council of Teachers of Mathematics.

———. 2005. *Navigating Through Problem Solving and Reasoning in Grade 4.* Reston, VA: National Council of Teachers of Mathematics.

Why Are Student Activities on a CD?

At first glance, the CD included with this book appears to be a collection of teaching tools and student activities, much like the activities that appear in many teacher resource books. But rather than taking a book to the copier to copy an activity, the CD allows you to simply print off the desired page on your home or work computer. No more standing in line at the copier or struggling to carefully position the book on the copier so you can make a clean copy. And with our busy schedules, we appreciate having activities that are classroom ready, and aligned with our math standards.

You may want to simplify some tasks or add complexity to others. The problems on the CD often include several parts or have added challenge extensions. When it is appropriate for your students, simply delete these sections, for a quick way to simplify or shorten the tasks. Remember to rename the file when saving it to preserve the integrity of the original activity. Here are some examples of ways you may want to change the tasks and why. A more complete version of this guide with more samples for editing the activities can be found on the CD-ROM.

Editing the CD to Motivate and Engage Students

Personalizing Tasks or Capitalizing on Students' Interests

The editable forms on the CD provide a quick and easy way to personalize math problems. Substituting students' names, the teacher's name, a favorite restaurant, sports team, or location can immediately engage students.

You know the interests of your students. Mentioning their interests in your problems is a great way to increase their enthusiasm for the activities. Think about their favorite activities and simply substitute their interests for those that might appear in the problems. In the second version of the example that follows, the teacher knows that many of her students play soccer and decides to reword the task to capture their interest.

Note: This type of editing is also important when the problem situation may not be culturally appropriate for your students (i.e., your students may not be engaged in Boy Scouting).

Name _____

The Boy Scout Breakfast

The Boy Scouts were planning a breakfast in the school gym. There were 5 round tables and 4 square tables. 6 people can sit at each round table and 4 people can sit at each square table. How many people can sit at all of the tables?

_____

Show your work.

Explain how you solved the problem.

_____
_____
_____
_____
_____
_____

Challenge: If every seat was filled for the breakfast and the cook made 3 pancakes for each person, how many pancakes did they need to cook for the breakfast? Show your work below and then explain how you got your answer on the back of this page.

Name _____

The Soccer Breakfast

The Rockville Soccer Stars were planning a breakfast in the school gym to raise money for new team uniforms. There were 5 round tables and 4 square tables. 6 people can sit at each round table and 4 people can sit at each square table. How many people can sit at all of the tables?

_____

Show your work.

Explain how you solved the problem.

_____
_____
_____
_____
_____

Challenge: If every seat was filled for the breakfast and the cook made 3 pancakes for each person, how many pancakes did they need to cook for the breakfast? Show your work and explain how you got your answer on the back of this page.

Editing the CD to Differentiate Instruction

Creating Shortened or Tiered Tasks

While many students are able to move from one task to another, some students benefit from focusing on one task at a time. By simply separating parts of a task teachers can help focus students on the first part of the task before moving them to part two. Teachers might choose to provide all students with the first task and then give students the second part after they have completed it and had their work checked by the teacher. In this sample, in which the two parts of the task initially appeared on one page together, the tasks have been separated and the lines for writing responses are wide for students who may need more writing space.

Name _____

Gathering Eggs

1. Kyle and Laura were playing a new video game in which they had to gather eggs in a basket. Kyle noticed that in the easy level of the game, the first egg earned him two points, the second egg earned four points, the third egg earned six points, and so on. How much did the eighth egg earn?

Describe the pattern that helped you solve the problem.

Name _____

Gathering Eggs

2. Laura reached the second level of the game, which was much harder! She had to gather golden eggs for her basket. She noticed that at this level, the first golden egg earned two points, the second golden egg earned four points, the third golden egg earned eight points, and the fourth golden egg earned sixteen points. How much did the eighth golden egg earn?

Describe the pattern that helped you solve the problem.

Modifying the Readability of Tasks

Adding some fun details can generate interest and excitement in story problems, but you might prefer to modify some problems for students with limited reading ability. Simply deleting some of the words on the editable CD will result in an easy-to-read version of the same task.

Name _____

Healthy Habits

Mrs. Birch's class was studying health and fitness. Every student decided on a plan to get healthier.

1. Danny decided to get more exercise. He rode his bike 2 miles each day for 9 days. How many miles did he ride?

_____

Show your work.

2. Kathy decided to eat less candy. She ate 21 pieces of candy last month and only 9 pieces of candy this month. How much fewer candy did she eat this month?

_____

Show your work.

3. Lisa decided to drink 3 glasses of milk each day. How many glasses of milk did she drink in a week?

_____

Show your work.

Explain how you figured out how much milk Lisa drank in a week.

_____
_____
_____

Name _____

Healthy Habits

1. Danny rode his bike 2 miles each day for 9 days. How many miles did he ride?

_____

Show your work.

2. Kathy ate 21 pieces of candy last month and only 9 pieces of candy this month. How much fewer candy did she eat this month?

_____

Show your work.

3. Lisa drank 3 glasses of milk each day. How many glasses of milk did she drink in a week?

_____

Show your work.

Explain how you got your answer.

_____
_____
_____

Modifying Data

While all students may work on the same problem task, modifying the problem data will allow teachers to create varying versions of the task. Using the editable forms on the CD, you can either simplify the data or insert more challenging data including larger numbers, fractions, decimals, or percents.

Name _____

Scoring Baskets

1. Brian scored 16 points in the first basketball game of the season. He scored 13 points in the second, 9 points in the third, and 10 points in the fourth. What was his scoring average for the first four games of the season?

_____

Show your work.

Explain how you solved the problem.

_____
_____
_____
_____
_____

2. If Brian scored 7 points in his next game, what would be his average for the first five games of the season? Explain how you figured it out.

_____
_____
_____
_____
_____

Name _____

Scoring Baskets

1. Brian scored 16 points in the first basketball game of the season. He scored 13 points in the second, 15 points in the third, 10 points in the fourth, and 11 points in the 5th game. What was his scoring average for the first five games of the season?

_____

Show your work.

Explain how you solved the problem.

_____
_____
_____
_____

2. If Brian scored 5 points in each of his next three games, what would be his average for the first eight games of the season? Explain how you figured it out.

_____
_____
_____
_____